Mācī-Anihšināpēmowin
Beginning Saulteaux

L. LYNN COTE | MARGARET R. COTE

University of Regina Press

COVER AND TEXT DESIGN: Duncan Campbell, University of Regina Press
INTERIOR LAYOUT: John van der Woude, JVDW Designs
PROOFREADER: Donna Grant
COVER ART: Robert Houle, *Morning Star*, 1976, acrylic on canvas, 121 x 151 cm, Indigenous Art Centre, Indigenous and Northern Affairs Canada, Gatineau.

Library and Archives Canada Cataloguing in Publication

Title: Mācī-anihšināpēmowin = Beginning Saulteaux / L. Lynn Cote, Margaret R. Cote.
Other titles: Beginning Saulteaux
Names: Cote, L. Lynn, 1965, author. | Cote, Margaret R., author.
Identifiers: Canadiana (print) 20200413627 | Canadiana (ebook) 20200413805 | ISBN 9780889777514 (spiral-bound) | ISBN 9780889777576 (hardcover) | ISBN 9780889777538 (PDF) | ISBN 9780889777552 (EPUB)
Subjects: LCSH: Ojibwa language—Study and teaching.
Classification: LCC PM851 .C68 2020 | DDC 497/.33380071—dc23

We acknowledge the support of the Canada Council for the Arts for our publishing program. We acknowledge the financial support of the Government of Canada. / Nous reconnaissons l'appui financier du gouvernement du Canada. This publication was made possible through Creative Saskatchewan's Book Publishing Production Grant Program, as well as the Canadian Heritage Indigenous Languages and Cultures Program, administered by the Saskatchewan Indigenous Cultural Centre in partnership with SaskCulture Inc.

This book is dedicated to the memory of nimihšōmihšipan
(my late grandfather) John F. Cote (1999) and nōhkōyipan
(my late grandmother) Madelaine M. Cote (1995).

CONTENTS

ACKNOWLEDGEMENTS

There are so many people to thank for their guidance, assistance, and expertise in raising me within the Anihšināpē language and culture. First, I would like to give thanks to kihci-manitō (Great Spirit), ninanāhkomā (I'm grateful to him/her) for giving me life and this beautiful language. Also to my late grandparents, nimihšōmihšipan (my late grandfather) John F. Cote and nōhkōyipan (my late grandmother) Madelaine Cote, ninanāhkomāk (I'm grateful to them) for teaching me the language and raising me with the traditional values and beliefs. Without them I would not have known and studied the language.

Ninanāhkomāk nitinawēmākanak (I'm thankful to all my relatives), nōhs (my father) Patrick Cote and nimāmāhkān (my step-mother) Elizabeth Yuzicappi-Cote for their support, guidance and teachings; nikāyipan (my late mother) Faye L. Cote for giving me life and speaking the language; nikosihsak (my sons) B.J., Gabriel, Tyler, and Justis for their patience and support; ninōhsēyēnsak (my grandchildren) Mikhye, Keiren, Torrin, Elexis, and Kiniw; nimihsē (my older sister) Norinne Cote and nihsīmē (my younger sibling) Dwayne Cote for their support and guidance; and to all my extended family that I was raised with.

Also, to nišikohš (my paternal aunt), my mentor, Margaret R. Cote for getting me interested in the language and for teaching me to understand how the language works. Without her knowledge and expertise this book would not have been possible, and also for co-publishing this text kinanāhkomin (I'm grateful to you).

I would like to extend my heartfelt gratitude to the many scholars who provided me with guidance and expertise through the writing of this text. To the scholars at First Nation University of Canada; Department of Language and Culture faculty: Margaret Cote (retired), the late Darren Okemaysim, Solomon Ratt, and Dr. Arok Wolvengrey. Without their academic expertise and knowledge I would not have been able to complete my research.

I am also grateful to the people at U of R Press, Kelly Laycock, Donna Grant, and John van der Woude, for their assistance in layout, in printing, and in helping me improve the text. And finally, to all those that have assisted me and have not been listed here, please accept my apologies and kihci-mīkwēc.

Mācī-Anihšināpēmowin: Beginning Saulteaux was written to address the need for a comprehensive working textbook for new students of the Saulteaux language and as a resource for Saulteaux language teachers teaching at a beginning level. The Indigenous Languages for Beginners series is set up for casual learners or independent students to learn at their own pace, as the lessons are easy to follow and the words are easy to pronounce using the spelling system found in this book.

The information and methods found within this text are taken from *Nahkawēwin* by Margaret Cote (1984) and the cumulation of my years teaching the Saulteaux language. They have been tested and used at the university level and have been quite effective for students and teachers. As a teacher of the Saulteaux language and as a university student studying the Saulteaux language, I have been able to make improvements that I found to be helpful. It is my hope that this textbook will be of help in assisting students to learn the Saulteaux language and, thus, retain and keep alive this language that has been slowly disappearing like so many other Indigenous languages in Canada and the United States. Saulteaux is an Algonquian language that is widespread across southern Canada and into northern and central United States. Speakers of other Algonquian languages from these areas will be able to find the relationship to their own languages within *Mācī-Anihšināpēmowin: Beginning Saulteaux.*

L. Lynn Cote
Regina, Saskatchewan
December 2020

INTRODUCTION

About the Saulteaux Language

The Saulteaux language is a language of many names. When it is recognized that Saulteaux, Ojibway, Ottawa, Chippewa, and Algonquin all refer to the same language, it is evident that this language is one of the most widely used North American Indigenous Languages. Communities where this language is spoken occur in the following areas:

- In the southern half of Saskatchewan and Manitoba, where the usual name of the language is *Saulteaux*.
- In Ontario, where the usual name is *Ojibway*, except around Manitoulin Island, where *Ottawa* or *Odawa* is the preferred name.
- In Western Quebec, where the usual name is *Algonquin*.
- In North Dakota, Minnesota, Wisconsin, and Michigan, where the usual name is *Chippewa*.

Any language that is spoken over a wide area for a long while develops regional differences in pronunciation, grammar and vocabulary. Saulteaux was already widely spoken in North America long before English was spoken here at all, so it is only natural that the regional variation in Saulteaux is greater than that of the English language. A Saskatchewan Saulteaux speaker might have difficulty understanding an Ontario Ojibway speaker.

The type of Saulteaux that is spoken in a given area is called the *dialect* of that area. The Saulteaux in this book, *Mācī-Anihšināpēmowin* by L. Lynn Cote and Margaret R. Cote, is the Saskatchewan dialect that is spoken in the area of Kamsack in southeastern Saskatchewan.

The Saulteaux language belongs to the Algonquian Language Family. Other languages that belong to the Algonquian Language Family are Cree, Montagnais, Maliseet, Passamaquoddy, Fox, Cheyenne, Blackfoot, Micmac, Potawatami, and Arapaho, among others.

First Nations Languages Spoken in Saskatchewan

There are five Indigenous languages spoken in Saskatchewan. These five languages belong to three linguistic groups.

Linguistic group	Language	Area spoken
Algonquian	Saulteaux	Southeastern Saskatchewan
	Cree (Swampy & Plains)	South & Central Saskatchewan
	Cree (Woods)	Northern Saskatchewan
Siouan	Dakota (Sioux)	Southern Saskatchewan
	Nakoda (Assiniboine)	Southern Saskatchewan
Athapaskan	Dene (Chipewayan)	Northern Saskatchewan

First Nations in Saskatchewan

There are seventy-four First Nations in Saskatchewan. The languages of these First Nations are as follows:

# of First Nations	Language	Dialect
44	Cree	Plains (Y), Swampy (N), Woods (TH)
15	Saulteaux	
7	Dene	Chipewayan
8	Dakota, Lakota Nakoda	Sioux Assiniboine

There are fifteen Saulteaux First Nations in Saskatchewan, each with minor variations in dialect (as shown in the table below). In some regions, Saulteaux is the dominant language, with Cree also being spoken in the area. In other areas, the Cree language has been adopted and has become the dominant language of the band. An example of this is Saulteaux First Nation. This may be the result of Saulteaux First Nation's geographical location: it is situated in northwestern Saskatchewan surrounded by Cree language groups.

First Nation	Language spoken	First Nation	Language spoken
Cote	Saulteaux	Cowessess	Saulteaux and Cree
Fishing Lake	Saulteaux	George Gordon	Saulteaux and Cree
Keeseekoose	Saulteaux	Pasqua	Saulteaux and Cree
Key	Saulteaux	Sakimay	Saulteaux and Cree
Kinistin	Saulteaux	Okanese	Cree and Saulteaux
Muskowekwan	Saulteaux	Saulteaux	Cree and Saulteaux
Muscowpetung	Saulteaux	White Bear	Cree and Saulteaux
Yellow Quill	Saulteaux		

Notes and Suggestions for the Student

As soon as a little bit of Saulteaux is known, the student should practise using it as often as possible. This will mean talking in Saulteaux about a lot of uninteresting things, and saying things in the Saulteaux language that one would not waste time saying in English. It can be very frustrating to adults to talk foolishness, but the aim of studying Saulteaux is, of course, to learn Saulteaux, not to make intellectual conversation. Most language learners are little children, learning their own mother language. Adults should come to language learning in the same way: they must learn to speak the language like a child before they can learn to speak it like an adult.

The intention of this book is to introduce the Saulteaux language, its grammatical structures and spelling system. The content in this book is merely the tip of the iceberg in regard to the complexity of the Saulteaux language.

Noted here are some of the things that learning a language includes:

- **Vocabulary:** It is obvious that the words of different languages are different; therefore, learning a new language requires learning many new words and memorizing their meanings.
- **Syntax:** Languages also differ from each other in less obvious ways. For example, the arrangement or order of words to make sentences, called *syntax*, differs across

languages. Therefore, the rules of syntax must also be learned when learning a new language.

- **Affixes:** In many languages, meanings are not represented only by whole words, but also by sounds or syllables attached to other words. Such sounds and syllables are called *affixes*. An English example of an affix is the *s* in *dogs*, *hats*, and *bones*, which makes the words plural, but which is a meaningless hiss or buzz when spoken alone. When an affix is attached to the end of a word, it is called a suffix. The *s* in the examples above is a *plural suffix*. When an affix is attached to the beginning of a word, it is called a prefix. The *un-* in *untidy* or *unused* is a prefix. Affixes, their meanings, and their uses differ greatly from language to language and must be learned anew in a new language, including the Saulteaux language.
- **Orthography:** *Orthography* is a spelling system. The spelling system used in this book is a phonetic alphabet; that is, it is designed to indicate pronunciation in a consistent way.
- **Phonology:** *Phonology* is the study of sounds. In learning a new language, the language learner imitates the teacher's pronunciation. Each language features, for example, particular vowel sounds, various articulations of consonants, and rules for accented or non-accented syllables.
- **Grammar:** *Grammar* concerns how words relate to one another to provide meaning. Grammatical terms include the parts of speech, such as nouns, pre-nouns, pronouns, particles, pre-verbs and verbs. The student should try to memorize every Saulteaux word, phrase, and sentence in this course, for it is much easier to learn to use the affixes and word arrangements, or syntax, of a language when examples of them are memorized.

Learning a language is very difficult and is only possible with the assistance of a teacher. In other words, *the student must expend most of the effort and strive to remember the Saulteaux words, phrases, and sentences.* There is no way for any teacher or any machine to put a language into the student's head without the student's own hard work. Fortunately, the human brain is designed to learn language. Remember, though, that a classroom is not the best place to learn a language. The best place to learn a language is in the natural environment.

People who are learning Saulteaux should always let their ears be their guide (not their eyes), and people should try to repeat what they *hear*. Instructors of Saulteaux should always say what they feel is right and never let what is written lead them astray from good, natural, colloquial Saulteaux.

CHAPTER
· · · · · · · · · · ·
1

Objectives

- Spelling and sound system of Saulteaux
- Grammatical terms
- Abbreviations

Saulteaux Spelling and Sounds

Orthography is a spelling system and *phonology* is the study of sounds. The spelling system used in this book is a phonetic alphabet; that is, it is designed to indicate pronunciation in a consistent way. But it must be remembered that human beings are designed to learn languages by imitating spoken words, not marks on paper. So the only way for a student to learn to pronounce Saulteaux words is to imitate the teacher's pronunciation.

The teacher should pronounce every Saulteaux word, phrase, and sentence in a natural way and at a natural speed. Students should listen carefully and imitate what they hear. Students often ask a teacher to "say it slowly." The teacher may help students in this way as long as students are taught to say the word or phrase at the normal speed as well.

The material in this book is organized in an order that makes the learning of Saulteaux as efficient and easy as possible, and it offers explanations of Saulteaux grammar and cultural context.

THE ORTHOGRAPHY

The orthography used in this textbook is the Standard Roman Orthography (SRO), which is based on the Roman alphabet. There are 14 letters of the Roman alphabet used in Saulteaux spelling: *a, c, e, h, i, k, m, n, o, p, s, t, w,* and *y.* These 14 letters are used to represent 18 sounds, but if the *allophones* (one sound that is pronounced differently in different contexts) are included, there are a total of 24 sounds, including the consonant clusters and combinations. Please note that square brackets [ ] will be used to represent sounds in text, while slant lines // will be used to set apart spelling. *Italics* will be used for words used as words and letters as letters in text, while **bold** will present new terms in text.

The principles of Saulteaux spelling are:

1. Every sound has its own symbol

fortis (strong) [p] sound is represented by /p/	a**p**in	*sit*
lenis (weak) [p] sound is represented by /hp/	pā**hp**in	*laugh*

2. Each symbol represents only one sound

fortis /p/ represents the [p] sound	a**p**in
lenis /hp/ represents the [ʔp] sound	pā**hp**in

3. A single sound is written with a single letter

/š/ represents the [zh] sound	pē**š**ik	*one*
/hš/ represents the [sh] sound	šī**hš**īp	*a duck*

The principles of Saulteaux word structure are:

1. Every word begins with either a vowel (e.g., **a**pi *she/he is sitting*); a single consonant (e.g., **p**āhpi *she/he is laughing*); or a consonant followed by w (e.g., **pw**ānihšimo *she/he is dancing powwow*).

2. There are no combinations of vowels; vowels must be separated by an /h/ (e.g., masina**h**ikan *a book*) and no words begin with an /h/.

Saulteaux has a *somewhat* free word order. The English language has a fixed word order: the subject comes before the verb and object (SVO). In Saulteaux the word order is not so rigid. For example, each of the four sentences below has the subject, verb, and object in a different order, but all of the sentences mean *My mother bought meat.*

Nimāmā kī-atāwē wīyāhs.	Wīyāhs kī-atāwē nimāmā.
S **V** **O**	**O** **V** **S**

Kī-atāwē wīyāhs nimāmā.	Kī-atāwē nimāmā wīyāhs.
V **O** **S**	**V** **S** **O**

THE PHONOLOGY

Vowels

The Saulteaux language uses four vowels of the Roman alphabet: *a*, *i*, *o*, and *e*. These four vowels represent seven sounds, three short vowels sounds and four long ones. The three short vowels—*a*, *i*, and *o*—are spelled *without* a macron and are spoken quickly. The four long vowels—*ā*, *ī*, *ō*, and *ē*—are spelled *with* a macron and are spoken slowly.

Short Vowel Sounds (with examples in the Initial, Medial, and Final Position)							
Short vowel	**Initial position**		**Medial position**		**Final position**		**(closest) English counterpart**
a	**a**pin	*sit*	nak**a**mon	*sing*	wīp**a**	*soon*	**a**pparent
i	**i**hkwē	*woman*	ap**i**n	*sit*	maw**i**	*she/he is crying*	**i**nside
o	**o**nākan	*dish*	pim**o**hsēn	*walk*	kēk**o**	*don't*	**o**pinion

Long Vowel Sounds (with examples in the Initial, Medial, and Final Position)							
Long vowel	**Initial position**		**Medial position**		**Final position**		**(closest) English counterpart**
ā	**ā**nīn	*how*	m**ā**c**ā**n	*leave*	kēk**ā**	*almost*	p**a**pa
ī	**ī**witi	*over there*	k**ī**n	*you*	cīkah**ī**	*beside*	**I**roquois
ō	**ō**cīns	*housefly*	n**ō**nkom	*today*	kēk**ō**	*something*	b**oo**t
ē	**ē**nikōns	*ant*	t**ē**w**ē**hikan	*drum*	mīnank**ē**	*yes*	b**e**rry

The vowel /e/ is always long in Saulteaux; therefore, it is always written with a macron *ē*. If the words were to be spelled with double vowels to indicate the long sound, then the words that are long would be even longer and more difficult to read.

otāpānāhkōk *wagons*
otaapaanaahkook

There is no [ɛ] vowel sound in Saulteaux as in *elf* or *bet*, and there is no [æ] vowel sound as in *apple* or *bat*. Also, there are not very many words in the Saulteaux language that begin with a long i → ī.

Saulteaux has an additional vowel sound that occurs only in certain environments. When *wā* occurs at the beginning of a word, as in the words *wāpōs* "rabbit" and *wāhsa* "far," it has the standard long [a:] sound. However, when *wā* follows a consonant in the middle of a word, as in the examples below, it is pronounced [ɔ:], as in the English words "paw," "saw," and "cot."

hwā	opahkitē**hwā**n	*she/he hits him/her/it*
kwā	iš**kwā**ntēm	*a door*
twā	niko**twā**hso	*six*
nwā	nā**nwā**pik	*five dollars*
pwā	oh**pwā**kan	*a sacred pipe*
šwā	nī**šwā**hso	*seven*
swā	nih**swā**hso	*eight*
mwā	a**mwā**tā	*let's eat it* (animate direct object)

The diagram below represents the mouth cavity, showing where the tongue is positioned in the vocal tract to produce the vowel sounds in any language. This diagram shows the vowel sounds in Saulteaux. For the vowel sound [ī], for example, the tongue is at the *front* of the mouth close to the front teeth and is placed *high* at the roof of the mouth. In contrast, the [ā] sound is produced with the tongue relaxed *low* in the mouth and more *central*.

Tongue Placement for Proper Vowel Pronunciation in Saulteaux			
	Front	**Central**	**Back**
High	ī i		o
Mid	ē		ō ([c]wā)*
Low		a ā	

Consonants

The 10 consonants, *c, h, k, m, n, p, s, t, w,* and *y,* are used to represent 18 sounds and a number of consonant clusters. Counting allophones, there are a total of 24 sounds. The following linguistic terms will help you understand how the sounds are made within the mouth.

Place of articulation:

- **bilabial**: the lower lip articulates against the upper lip
- **alveolar**: the tip of the tongue articulates against the alveolar ridge (just behind the top teeth)
- **alveopalatal**: the blade of the tongue articulates against the roof of the mouth in the space behind the alveolar ridge bordering the palate
- **palatal**: the front of the tongue articulates against the palate

....

* When a long *ā* follows a *w*, the consonant [c] preceding the *wā* will change the the sound of the vowel.

- **velar**: the back of the tongue articulates against the velum (the soft palate at the back of the throat)
- **glottal**: the vocal folds deep in the throat are held closed so no air escapes, while the mouth remains open, as heard in the English expression, "Uh-oh."

Manner of articulation:

- **obstruents**: a class of sounds that involve an obstruction, including stops, affricates, and fricatives
- **sonorants**: a class of sounds that involve continuous sound, including nasals, glides, and vowels
- **stops/plosives**: sounds that involve a complete closure so that no air escapes the mouth
- **affricates**: sounds that involve sequences of stop plus fricative
- **fricatives**: sounds made with a small opening, allowing air to escape with some friction
- **nasals**: sounds that allow air to pass through the nose
- **glides**: sounds that function like consonants but are phonetically like moving vowels
- **aspiration**: a period of voicelessness following a consonant

Consonants in SRO								
Place of articulation/ Manner of articulation			**Bilabial**	**Alveolar**	**Alveo- palatal**	**Palatal**	**Velar**	**Glottal**
Obstruents	Stops/ Plosives	fortis	hp	ht			hk	h
		lenis	p	t			k	
	Affricates	fortis			hc			
		lenis			c			
	Fricatives	fortis		hs	hš			
		lenis		s	š			(h)
Sonorants	Nasals	+voiced	m	n			(n)	
	Glides	+voiced				y	w	

The three consonants *p*, *t* and *k* are stop phonemes (a **phoneme** is a contrasting segment in a language) and have the phonetic features of being fortis (strong) and pre-aspirated, and lenis (weak) and un-aspirated. The following table shows examples of the three stop phonemes and their allophones. An **allophone** is a morphologically or phonologically conditioned variant of a phoneme, and its distribution is predictable.

Stop Phonemes and Allophones

Phoneme	Allophone & features	Saulteaux		(closest) English counterpart
/p/	[p] – fortis, pre-aspirated	apin	*sit*	**b**ig
	[hp] – lenis, un-aspirated	pāhpin	*laugh*	ha**pp**y
/t/	[t] – fortis, pre-aspirated	pītōn	*bring it*	**t**one
	[ht] – lenis, un-aspirated	kišāhtē	*it's hot*	si**tt**ing
/k/	[k] – fortis, pre-aspirated	kēko	*don't*	**g**o
	[hk] – lenis, un-aspirated	kahkina	*everyone, all*	su**ck**

The consonant *c* is an affricate phoneme and has the phonetic features of being fortis (strong) and pre-aspirated, and lenis (weak) and un-aspirated. The following table shows an example of the affricate phoneme and its allophones.

Affricate Phonemes and Allophones

Phoneme	Allophone & features	Saulteaux		(closest) English counterpart
/c/	[č] – fortis, pre-aspirated	mīcin	*eat it*	ma**j**or
	[hč] – lenis, un-aspirated	pihcīnāko	*yesterday*	**ch**ip

The consonants *s* and *hs* are fricative phonemes and also have the phonetic features of fortis (strong) and pre-aspirated, and lenis (weak) and un-aspirated. The following table shows examples of the fricative phonemes and their allophones.

Fricative Phonemes and Allophones

Phoneme	Allophone & features	Saulteaux		(closest) English counterpart
/s/	[z] – fortis, pre-aspirated	kinōsē	*jackfish*	ea**s**y
	[s] – lenis, un-aspirated	wāhsa	*far*	e**ss**ay
/š/	[ž] – fortis, pre-aspirated	pēšik	*one*	trea**s**ure
	[š] – lenis, un-aspirated	šīhšīp	*a duck*	**sh**ip

All the aforementioned consonants are lenis and un-aspirated at the beginning of a word.

In the Saulteaux language the consonant *h* is almost always silent. The *h* is only pronounced in Saulteaux interjections, as the following examples:

ahām	*okay*
wāhowa	*geez*
īhay	*expression of fear*
yoho	*expression of surprise*

The other uses of the *h* are as follows:

a) separates 2 vowels:

masinahikan	*book*

b) distinguishes the voiceless consonants:

pītōn	*bring it*
pī**ht**ōn	*wait for it*

c) is used as a glottal stop:

mina**h**	*give him a drink*
wīci**h**	*help him/her*

When a suffix is added, the *h* becomes silent again, as in the following words:

pī**h**ātā	*let's wait for him/her*
nipōni**h**āk	*I am leaving them alone*

The Saulteaux consonants *m* and *n* (nasals, voiced) and *w* and *y* (glides, voiced) have similar sounds as in the English language, as the following table indicates. When these consonants stand alone between vowels, they regularly have the voiced sound.

Initial, Medial, and Final Vowel Sounds							
Consonant	Initial position		Medial position		Final position		(closest) English counterpart
/m/	**m**ōhkomān	*knife*	kē**m**ā	*or*	mištati**m**	*horse*	**m**an
/n/	**n**ōnkom	*today*	ini**n**i	*man*	ahsi**n**	*a rock*	**n**ame
/w/	**w**īyāhs	*meat*	nī**w**in	*four*	nōnta**w**	*hear him/her*	**w**ay
/y/	**y**oho	*expression of surprise*	awi**y**a	*someone*	nita**y**	*my dog/ pet*	**y**es

Saulteaux also has nine voiced consonant clusters, as seen below.

Cluster	Saulteaux		Sound	(closest) English counterpart
/mp/	ampē	come	/p/ pronounced as [+b] after m	umbrella
/nt/	ānti	where	/t/ pronounced as [+d] after n	under
/nc/	onincīn	his/her hand	/c/ pronounced as [+j] after n	injure
/nk/	wāpank	tomorrow	/k/ pronounced as [+g] after n	lung
/ns/	mōnsōk	moose (pl)	/s/ pronounced as nasal	loans
/nš/	onšām	because	/š/ pronounced as nasal	no close sound
/šp/	išpimink	up/above	/šp/ pronounced [shp]	no close sound
/št/	oštikwān	his/her head	/šk/ pronounced [sht]	no close sound
/šk/	pāškišikan	a gun	/šk/ pronounced [shk]	no close sound

A consonant after *m* or *n* will also be a voiced consonant. After a long vowel and before *s* or *š*, the *n* is not pronounced; it becomes a nasalized sound.

Pronunciation
Accented syllables, in any language, are the syllables that are stressed, that is, pronounced more prominently than others. In the English language, words with the same spelling but different meaning are sometimes distinguished by having different syllables stressed, or accented. For example:

cóntract	contráct	cóntest	contést
cónflict	conflíct	réfuse	refúse
cónverse	convérse	pérmit	permít

In Saulteaux, words are not distinguished in this way. Whether a syllable is accented is determined by the vowels in the syllable and the position of the word in a sentence. In Saulteaux, each vowel forms a separate syllable. The following syllables are accented:

1. Each syllable with a long vowel.

2. The last syllable of each word.

3. Every second syllable in a sequence of syllables containing short vowels.

Most Saulteaux speakers drop unaccented short vowels. The short vowels *a* and *i* are especially omitted between *m* and *p*, between *n*, *t*, *c*, or *k*, and before the fortis consonants *p*, *t*, *c*, *k*, *s*, and *š*. In the examples below, the omitted letter is represented by the apostrophe (') in the Pronunciation column, while the stressed syllable is indicated by the accent symbol (´).

Spelling		Pronunciation
pimipahtōn	*run*	pimíp'htō´n
kipimipahtō	*you are running*	kipím'pahtō´
nikosihsak	*my sons*	n'kós'hśak
mawatihšiwē	*she/he is visiting*	mawát'hšiwē´

Note how the presence or absence of a personal prefix, *ni-* or *ki-*, causes the accented syllables to vary. Slow, careful speakers may not drop out these short vowels.

Many people also omit the *w*, *y*, and the short vowel *i* in rapid speech, as seen below.

Spelling		Pronunciation (rapid speech)
niwāpamā	*I see him*	ni'apama
ānti ēšāyēk	*where are you* (pl) *going*	ānti ēšā'ēk
kīwēn	*go home*	kī'ēn
kāwīn kēkō	*nothing*	kā'n kēkō
kāwīn mahsi	*not yet*	kā'mahsi
nikīwē	*I'm going home*	n'kīwē
nipimohsē	*I'm walking*	m'pimohsē
nipāpā	*my father*	m'pāpā
nitanohkī	*I'm working*	n'tanohkī

The existence of these two forms—a slow, careful form with the *w*, *y* and *i*, and a rapid or collapsed form without the *w*, *y* and *i*—is similar to certain contractions in English, such as:

I'm	I am	You're	You are
don't	do not	I'm gonna go	I am going to go
I dunno	I do not know	Jeet jet?	Did you eat yet?

Although English words are used here to provide comparisons for learning the pronunciation of Saulteaux words, it is important to note that English spelling rules are far more irregular than the spelling rules for the Saulteaux language. Note the different sounds in these English examples:

ea	b**ea**r, d**ea**d, **ea**r, h**ea**rt, r**ea**d, y**ea**h, s**ea**, l**ea**ve, l**ea**ven
ough	b**ough**, c**ough**, en**ough**, th**ough**, thr**ough**, hicc**ough**, sl**ough**

In the sentence below, note how the [ī] sound is spelled in eleven different ways:

> Did he believe that Caesar could see the people seize the seas, while the silly amoeba stole the key from the machine?

The word *ghoti* could be used to spell *fish* if English rules of spelling are used. For example, the /gh/ as the [f] sound in enough, /o/ as the [i] sound in women, and the /ti/ as the [sh] sound in nation.

In the Saulteaux language, the phonetic alphabet means that spelling and pronunciation follow consistent rules.

Grammatical Terms

Understanding grammar is an important part of learning any language. This section lists the grammatical terms that will be used in this course book.

The parts of speech in Saulteaux, as in other languages, include nouns, pre-nouns, pronouns, particles, pre-verbs and verbs. The reason for placing verbs last on the list is that they are very complex and very important; all the other parts of speech depend on the verbs, and nearly all the other parts of speech are capable of being put into a verbal form.

In forming a sentence in Saulteaux, it is the rule to employ a verb wherever possible; thus, the English sentence *He was at our last meeting* would be rendered in Saulteaux as *He was there when we last met.* The Saulteaux language does not make a distinction between gender *she/he*, when speaking about a male or female; this applies to the verb as well.

The peculiarities of the Saulteaux language will present themselves as you proceed to study the language, but here are a few points of anticipation:

- **noun:** a person, place, thing, or idea
  - **gender of nouns:** The Saulteaux language divides all nouns into two categories: animate and inanimate, rather than masculine and feminine.
  - **noun types:** The Saulteaux language has diminutive, locative, pejorative, compound, possessive, and dependent nouns.
- **number:** refers to one, singular (sg), or more than one, plural (pl)
- **obviation:** animate and inanimate noun obviation, a distinction made between third persons in a given context
- **particles and pre-verbs:** used to add additional information to a verb or phrase
- **pre-noun:** adds information to a noun
- **pronoun:** a word used instead of a noun. The Saulteaux language has personal pronouns, interrogative pronouns, and demonstrative pronouns.

- **tense/aspect:** tense indicates a time of an action, state, or event; aspect considers qualities of an action or state, independent of tense
- **verb:** describes an action, state, or event
    - **verb types:** Four types of verbs are discussed in this book: inanimate intransitive (V-II), animate intransitive (V-AI), transitive inanimate (V-TI), and transitive animate (V-TA).
    - **mode types:** Mode indicates the intention of the speaker. This book covers indicative, negative indicative, imperative, negative imperative, delayed imperative, subjunctive, and negative subjunctive.

Abbreviations

You will find the following abbreviations used throughout this book:

- c – consonant
- ex – exclusive
- in – inclusive
- NA – animate noun
- NI – inanimate noun
- PC – particle
- pl – plural
- PN – pronoun
- PV – pre-verb
- sg – singular
- V-AI – animate intransitive verb
- V-II – inanimate intransitive verb
- V-TA – transitive animate verb
- V-TI – transitive inanimate verb

For practise with the Saulteaux vowels and consonants, see the Chapter 1 Exercises on pages 149–150.

CHAPTER

· · · · · · · · · · ·

2

Objectives

- Minimal pairs and near-minimal pairs
- Greetings and polite responses

Dialogues

1. Ānīn šikwa kīn?
   Kāwīn kotinō, kīn tahs?
   Pēšikwan.

   How are you now?
   Nothing's wrong, you then?
   The same.

2. Ānīn šikwa kimāmā.
   Mino-ayā. Mīkwēc.
   Kipāpā tahs, mino-ayā na?
   Mīnankē. / Kāwīn.

   How is your mother?
   She is fine. Thanks.
   Your father then, is he fine?
   Yes. / No.

3. Kika-wāpamin mīnawā.
   Mīnankē, kika-wāpamin mīnawā.

   I'll see you again.
   Yes, I'll see you again.

4. Ānīn šikwa kīnawā?
   Kāwīn kotinō, kīnawā tahs?
   Kika-wāpamininim mīnawā.

   How are you people now?
   Nothing's wrong, you people then?
   I'll see you all again.

Vocabulary

Ānīn šikwa kīn?	*Hello, Hi,* or *How are you?*
Kāwīn kotinō.	*Nothing is wrong.*
Kika-wāpamin mīnawā.	*I'll see you again.*
Ānīn šikwa ēši-ayāyan?	*How are you feeling now?*
Nimino-ayā.	*I am fine/well.*

Minimal Pairs and Near-Minimal Pairs

In the Saulteaux language there are quite a few words that look and sound alike. These are called **minimal pairs** and **near-minimal pairs**.

Minimal pairs are two words that are almost identical except for *one* sound difference. Below are some examples of minimal pairs.

Minimal Pairs			
Saulteaux	**English**	**Saulteaux**	**English**
sākahamok	*go outside* (pl)	kāwīn	*no*
sākahamōk	*they're going outside*	kāwēn	*be jealous* (sg)
pōni-	*to stop*	kišišihtē	*she/he has hot feet*
pōnī	*she/he lands*	kišišihkē	*she/he makes it hot (fire)*
pītōn	*bring it* (sg)	otayan	*his/her dog (pet)*
pīhtōn	*wait for it* (sg)	otayān	*she/he has it*
ahsēmā	*tobacco*	antotamok	*listen* (pl)
ahsamā	*she/he's being fed*	antotamōk	*they're listening*
akim	*count him/her/it* (sg)	anohkī	*she/he is working*
ākim	*snowshoe*	anōhkī	*she/he asks s.o. to work for him/her*
sākahikan	*lake*	miskwi	*blood*
sakahikan	*nail/brad*	miskwā	*it is red*
mihtikōn	*sticks*	nīpīns	*a leaf*
mihtikōk	*trees*	nipīns	*a little water*
sīpi	*a river*	pāhpi	*she/he is laughing*
sīpī	*she/he stretches*	pāhpih	*laugh at him/her/it* (sg)

Saulteaux	English	Saulteaux	English
pakān	peanut	nōtin	it is windy
pahkān	different	nātin	fetch it (sg)
akihk	nasal mucus/snot	opwāmān	she/he can't convince him/her
ahkihk	a pail/kettle	opwāman	his/her thighs
mišihsē	a turkey	kīšpin nipāyān	If I sleep...
nišihsē	my father-in-law	kīšpin nipāyan	If you sleep...
ocākišān	she/he burns it	pankitōn	be quiet (sg)
ocākišwān	she/he burns him/her/it	mankitōn	big mouth

Near-minimal pairs are two or more words that have *more than one* sound difference. Listed below are some near-minimal pairs and sets.

Near-Minimal Pairs & Sets			
Saulteaux	English	Saulteaux	English
amo	eat it (NA*) (sg)	kēko	don't
āmō	a bee	kēkō	something
ōtēnānk	in/to/at/by town	kīkō	a fish
otānānk	behind	kīšihtē	it is cooking
nimīnā	I give it to him/her/it	kišihtē	it is hot (indoors)
niminahā	I give him/her/it a drink	kišāhtē	it is hot (outdoors)
maci-	bad/evil	tipihkat	it is night
mācī-	to start	tipihkahk	tonight
		tipihkonk	last night

In these words, the sound differences are either vowels or consonants. This is why it is important to know the Saulteaux sound system: one sound, either vowel or consonant, can change the meaning of the word.

To practise what you've learned so far, choose five minimal or near-minimal pairs from the chart above and take your time pronouncing them aloud. Make sure to go slowly enough

* NA stands for Noun Animate, meaning that *it* refers to an animate noun.

to distinguish the sounds that are different in each pair or group. Write your list down and make sure the macrons are in the correct places.

Greetings and Polite Responses

- *Ānīn šikwa kīn* is a greeting that can be used as an equivalent to "Hello," "Hi," and "How are you?" The literal meaning is "How now you?"

- *Kāwīn kotinō* "nothing is wrong" is usually shortened to *kān kotinō* or *kān kot*. The literal meaning of *kotinō* is "something," so when it's negated (*kāwīn* preceding the word) it means "nothing." This is the most common response to *ānīn šikwa kīn*.

- *Kika-wāpamin mīnawā* "I'll see you again" is the most commonly used equivalent of *goodbye* in the Saulteaux language. There is no word for goodbye, so upon parting people usually say, *Kika-wāpamin mīnawā*.

- If you are greeting someone who you know has been sick, you may want to ask *Ānīn šikwa ēši-ayāyan?* "How are you feeling now?," but this is in regard to health, not things in general. The most common response would be *Nimino-ayā* "I am fine/well."

- *Šikwa* is a particle that can mean "and" or "now," depending on the context in which it is used:

with a command (imperative)	Wīhsinin **šikwa**.	*You* (sg) *eat* ***now***.
	Wīhsinik **šikwa**.	*You* (pl) *eat* ***now***.
in a statement (indicative)	Kihsinā **šikwa**.	*It is cold* ***now***.
between nouns	Animohš **šikwa** pōsīns wīhsiniwak.	*The dog* ***and*** *cat are eating.*

In English, the personal pronouns *you* (singular) and *you* (plural) are ambiguous (vague or unclear). English speakers make up for this deficiency by using *you guys*, *youse*, and *you all* as plurals for *you*. Saulteaux is much more specific about these personal pronouns:

kīn	*you* (sg)
kīnawā	*you* (pl)

An English-speaking person wanting to learn Saulteaux will have to keep these meanings separate and distinct.

- *Mīnankē* in Saulteaux is "yes," and there is also the interjection *ahām*, which has the meaning or expression "okay." *Taka* is another common expression, meaning "please." These expressions will be discussed in Chapter 7.

- *Mīkwēc* "thanks" is the informal way of thanking someone, but this expression would not be used in a formal situation such as thanking an Elder for giving advice or counselling. The more formal phrase *kinanāhkomin*, "I am grateful to you" or "I praise you," would be used.

Cultural note: It is a custom among First Nations people who know each other well to make themselves at home while visiting.

For practise, pair up with another student and take turns reading the dialogues at the beginning of the chapter as different speakers. Go over the dialogues several times.

For extra practise, see the Chapter 2 Exercises on page 151.

CHAPTER

· · · · · · · · · · ·

3

Objectives

- Akintāhsowinan (Numbers)
- Šōniyā (Money)
- Adding and subtracting

Dialogues

1. Ānīn šikwa kīn? — *How are you now?*
   Kān kotinō, kīn tahs? — *Nothing's wrong, you then?*
   Nimino-ayā. — *I'm fine.*

2. Taka awīhihšin šōniyā? — *Please lend me money?*
   Ānīn minik? — *How much?*
   Mitāhswāpik. — *Ten dollars.*
   Kāwīn onšām nīpawa. — *No, that's too much.*
   Nānwāpik tahs? — *Five dollars then?*
   Ahām. — *Okay.*
   Mīkwēc. — *Thanks.*

3. Ānahpī wā-tipāhamawiyan? — *When are you going to pay me?*
   Mākišā wāpank. — *Maybe tomorrow.*
   Ahām-ša, kika-wāpamin wāpank. — *Okay then, I'll see you tomorrow.*
   Mīnankē, kika-wāpamin wāpank. — *Yes, I'll see you tomorrow.*

Vocabulary

šōniyā	*money*
akintāhsowinan	*numbers*
otāhpinan	*minus* (literally, *take him/her/it*)
šikwa	*and/plus*
otāhpin	*minus* (lit., *take it*)
ānīn minik	*equals* (lit., *how much*)
pēšik šōniyāns	25¢ (lit., *one little money*)
nīš šōniyāns	50¢ (lit., *two little monies*)
nihso šōniyāns	75¢ (lit., *three little monies*)
pīwāpihkōns	*cents* (lit., *little metal*)
-wāpik	a suffix for money
ahsi	a particle used to connect numbers

Akintāhsowinan (Numbers)

kān kēkō	*zero* (lit., *nothing*)
pēšik	*one*
nīš	*two*
nihso	*three*
nīwin	*four*
nānan	*five*
nikotwāhso	*six*
nìśwāhso	*seven*
nihswāhso	*eight*
šānkahso	*nine*
mitāhso	*ten*

When counting higher than ten (10), the particle *ahsi* is used between the numbers.

mitāhso **ahsi** pēšik	*eleven*
mitāhso **ahsi** nīš	*twelve*
mitāhso **ahsi** nihso	*thirteen*
mitāhso **ahsi** nīwin	*fourteen*
mitāhso **ahsi** nānan	*fifteen*
mitāhso **ahsi** nikotwāhso	*sixteen*
mitāhso **ahsi** nīšwāhso	*seventeen*
mitāhso **ahsi** nihswāhso	*eighteen*
mitāhso **ahsi** šānkahso	*nineteen*
nīštana	*twenty*

Numbers by Tens		**Numbers by Hundreds**	
mitāhso	*ten*	nikotwāhk	*one hundred*
nīštana	*twenty*	nīšwāhk	*two hundred*
nihsomitana	*thirty*	nihswāhk	*three hundred*
nīmitana	*forty*	nīwāhk	*four hundred*
nānamitana	*fifty*	nānwāhk	*five hundred*
nikotwāhsomitana	*sixty*	nikotwāhswāhk	*six hundred*
nīšwāhsomitana	*seventy*	nīšwāhswāhk	*seven hundred*
nihswāhsomitana	*eighty*	nihswāhswāhk	*eight hundred*
šānkahsomitana	*ninety*	šānkahswāhk	*nine hundred*
nikotwāhk	*one hundred*	mitāhswāhk	*one thousand*

ADDING AND SUBTRACTING NUMBERS IN SAULTEAUX

Numbers can be added together in Saulteaux by using the particle *šikwa* for "and/plus." The particle *ānīn minik* (how much) is used as the equivalent to "equals." The following are examples of adding single- and dougle-digit numbers.

pēšik **šikwa** nīš, *ānīn minik?* nihso

1	+	2	=	3

nīštana **šikwa** mitāhso ahsi pēšik, *ānīn minik?* nihsomitana ahsi pēšik

20	+	11	=	31

Numbers can be subtracted in Saulteaux by using the transitive inanimate verb (V-TI) *otāhpin* (take it) as the equivalent to "minus." The following are examples of subtracting single- and double-digit numbers.

nānan **otāhpin** nīš, *ānīn minik?* nihso

5	–	2	=	3

nīštana **otāhpin** mitāhso ahsi pēšik, *ānīn minik?* šānkahso

20	–	11	=	9

Šōniyā (Money)

Money by Ones

pēšikwāpik	$1.00
nīšwāpik	$2.00
nihswāpik	$3.00
nīwāpik	$4.00
nānwāpik	$5.00
nikotwāhswāpik	$6.00
nīšwāhswāpik	$7.00
nihswāhswāpik	$8.00
šānkahswāpik	$9.00
mitāhswāpik	$10.00

Money by Tens

mitāhswāpik	$10.00
nīštana-tahswāpik	$20.00
nihsomitana-tahswāpik	$30.00
nīmitana-tahswāpik	$40.00
nānamitana-tahswāpik	$50.00
nikotwāhsomitana-tahswāpik	$60.00
nīšwāhsomitana-tahswāpik	$70.00
nihswāhsomitana-tahswāpik	$80.00
šānkahsomitana-tahswāpik	$90.00
nikotwāhk-tahswāpik	$100.00

Money by Hundreds

nīšwāhk-tahswāpik	$200.00
nihswāhk-tahswāpik	$300.00
nīwāhk-tahswāpik	$400.00
nānwāhk-tahswāpik	$500.00
mitāhswāhk-tahswāpik	$1000.00

Coins

pēšik šōniyāns	25¢ (lit., *one little money*)
nīš šōniyāns	50¢ (lit., *two little monies*)
nihso šōniyāns	75¢ (lit., *three little monies*)

The Saulteaux word used as an equivalent to "cents" is *pīwāpihkōns*.

pēšik pīwāpihkōns	1¢
nīš pīwāpihkōns	2¢
nihso pīwāpihkōns	3¢
nīwin pīwāpihkōns	4¢
nānan pīwāpihkōns	5¢
nikotwāhso pīwāpihkōns	6¢
nīšwāhso pīwāpihkōns	7¢
nihswāhso pīwāpihkōns	8¢
šānkahso pīwāpihkōns	9¢
mitāhso pīwāpihkōns	10¢

For higher amounts in cents, such as 11¢, the particle *ahsi* is used, as in the higher digits with numbers and money.

mitāhso ahsi pēšik pīwāpihkōns	11¢

ADDING AND SUBTRACTING MONEY IN SAULTEAUX

When adding money, dollars, and cents, *šikwa* is used, just as it is in the addition of numbers.

pēšik pīwāpihkōns **šikwa** nīš pīwāpihkōns, *ānīn minik?* nihso pīwāpihkōns

| 1¢ | + | 2¢ | = | 3¢ |

pēšikwāpik **šikwa** nīš pīwāpihkōns, *ānīn minik?* pēšikwāpik šikwa nīš pīwāpihkōns

| $1.00 | + | 2¢ | = | $1.02 |

pēšikwāpik **šikwa** nīšwāpik, *ānīn minik?* nihswāpik

| $1.00 | + | $2.00 | = | $3.00 |

When subtracting money, dollars, and cents, the transitive animate verb *otāhpinan* (take him/her/it) is used as the equivalent to "minus."

nīš pīwāpihkōns **otāhpinan** pēšik pīwāpihkōns, *ānīn minik?* pēšik pīwāpihkōns

| 2¢ | – | 1¢ | = | 1¢ |

pēšikwāpik **otāhpinan** nīš šōniyāns, *ānīn minik?* nīš šōniyāns *or* nānamitana pīwāpihkōns

| $1.00 | – | 50¢ | = | 50¢ |

nīšwāpik **otāhpinan** pēšikwāpik, *ānīn minik?* pēšikwāpik

| $2.00 | – | $1.00 | = | $1.00 |

For extra practise, see the Chapter 3 Exercises on page 152.

CHAPTER

• • • • • • • • • •

4

Objectives

- Introduction to nouns
- Gender classification
- Pluralization

Dialogues

1. Wēkonēn nōntaman?   *What do you hear?*
    Animohš ninōntawā.   *I hear a dog.*
    Iškotēw-otāpān ninōntān.   *I hear a train.*

2. Wēkonēn wāpantaman?   *What do you see?*
    Anankōk niwāpamāk.   *I see stars.*
    Wāhkāhikanan niwāpantānan.   *I see houses.*

Vocabulary

Animate (NA)		Inanimate (NI)	
ahkihk	*a pail/kettle*	atāwēwikamik	*a store*
ahsin	*a rock*	iškotē	*a fire*
āmō	*a bee*	masinahikan	*a book*

Animate (NA)		Inanimate (NI)	
animohš	*a dog*	nipi	*water*
apinōcī	*a child*	otāpān	*a car*
ēmihkwān	*a tablespoon*	otēhimin	*a strawberry*
kīsihs	*the sun*	sīpi	*a river*
mahīnkan	*a wolf*	tēhsitiyēpiwin	*a chair*
mahkwa	*a bear*	wāhkāhikan	*a house*
pinēhsī	*a bird*	wāpikwan	*a flower*

Introduction to Nouns

A noun is a person, place, thing, or idea. A **proper noun** is the name of a person or place, such as *Susan* or *Regina, Saskatchewan*. A **common noun** is the name of thing or idea, such as *dog* or *hope*. English uses the articles *a, an*, or *the* before a noun (*a* dog, *the* dog), but there are no such words in the Saulteaux language, so when translating a Saulteaux noun into English, don't forget to include the article.

The Saulteaux language has several types of nouns: diminutive, locative, pejorative, compound, possessive, and dependent. These will be discussed in more detail in Chapters 6 and 7.

In this chapter, we will discuss noun **gender**. Saulteaux nouns are divided into two gender categories: **animate** and **inanimate**.

Nouns can also be singular or plural in number. Saulteaux has a special process for pluralization called **affixation**, which will be discussed later in this chapter.

Gender Classification

Gender is a grammatical classification used to form agreement between nouns and other parts of speech. While approximately one quarter of the world's languages use a gender system, English nouns do not have grammatical gender. For example, the word *dog* in English does not distinguish whether it is a male or female animal. However, French and other Latin-based languages, for example, use masculine and feminine forms of the noun to distinguish gender: *un chien* (a male dog), *une chienne* (a female dog).

In Saulteaux, nouns are not distinguished by masculine or feminine classifiations but rather by their **animacy**. Animacy refers to living and non-living things.

Animate and *inanimate* are grammatical terms, and there are no hard-and-fast rules to determine whether a noun is animate or inanimate in Saulteaux. Some nouns were created to match the English language, and some nouns can be combined with verbs to create compound nouns. So don't get bogged down trying to figure out why something is considered alive when speaking about it in Saulteaux; just memorize the nouns that are animate and yet not really, such as *šōniyā* (money).

When you are in doubt about the animacy of a noun, you can check the Vocabulary List at the end of the book.

ANIMATE NOUNS

Most living things are classified as being animate, but there are many non-living items that also have the grammatical classification of being animate. Animate nouns include items that have a sacred use (culturally important items), most plant life, some anatomy, parts of the universe, and some personal items. The following list gives examples of some animate nouns.

animohš	*a dog*	oškans	*his/her fingernail*
ahsin	*a rock*	mitāhs	*pants*
kīkō	*a fish*	tipihki-kīsihs	*the moon*
ahsēmā	*tobacco*	ēmihkwān	*a spoon*
oškinīkīns	*a little boy*	ohpwākan	*a pipe*

INANIMATE NOUNS

Inanimate nouns are non-living objects, but this classification also includes some living things that *do not* fall in the animate category.

nipi	*water*	mōhkomān	*a knife*
otēhimin	*a strawberry*	wāpikwan	*a flower*
mahkisin	*a shoe*	sākahikan	*a lake*

Pluralization

In Saulteaux, singular means *one* and plural means *two or more*. To pluralize Saulteaux nouns an **affix** is attached to the noun. An affix is a small unit that has grammatical meaning that attaches to the *beginning, middle,* or *end* of a word. When it is attached at the beginning it is called a **prefix,** in the middle it is an **infix,** and at the end it is a **suffix.** The Saulteaux language has no infixes, but it does have prefixes and suffixes.

In Saulteaux, as in English, singular forms have no affixes and plural forms take affixes. For example, English nouns are pluralized by attaching the suffixes *-s* or *-es* to the end of a noun to mean two or more: dog (singular form) → dog**s** (plural form); glass (singular form) → glass**es** (plural form). In Saulteaux, as in English, *suffixes* are used to indicate the plural form, as in the following examples.

wāpōs	*a rabbit*	wāpōs**ōk**	*rabbits*
masinahikan	*a book*	masinahikan**an**	*books*

There are rules to pluralizing nouns in English, but in the Saulteaux language the plural forms for both animate and inanimate nouns take a variety of suffixes and do not follow any rules, so try to learn or memorize the plural endings as you encounter new nouns.

ANIMATE NOUN PLURAL SUFFIXES

Animate nouns can take different plural suffixes, as the following examples show. Note that all animate noun plural suffixes end with *-k*.

1. *-ōk*

Singular		Plural	
anank	*a star*	anank**ōk**	*stars*
mihtik	*a tree*	mihtik**ōk**	*trees*
ahkihk	*a pail*	ahkihk**ōk**	*pails*
otāpānāhk	*a wagon*	otāpānāhk**ōk**	*wagons*
kīsihs	*the sun*	kīsis**ōk**	*suns*

Some nouns such as *kīsihs* change in phonetics and form when the plural suffix is attached. In this word the weak *-hs* changes to the strong *-s*.

2. *-wak*

Singular		Plural	
inini	*a man*	inini**wak**	*men*
wašašk	*a muskrat*	wašašk**wak**	*muskrats*
ihkwē	*a woman*	ihkwē**wak**	*women*
āntēk	*a crow*	āntēk**wak**	*crows*
amihk	*a beaver*	amihk**wak**	*beavers*

This plural suffix is attached to nouns ending in both vowels and consonants.

3. *-yak*

Singular		Plural	
apinōcī	*a child*	apinōcī**yak**	*child**ren***
pinēhsī	*a bird*	pinēhsī**yak**	*birds*
wāpikanōcī	*a mouse*	wāpikanōcī**yak**	*mice*

These forms end in *-ī*, but not all nouns ending in this long vowel will take this plural suffix. For example, see *omahkahkī* "a frog" below.

4. *-k*

Singular		Plural	
āmō	*a bee*	āmō**k**	*bees*
mahkwa	*a bear*	mahkwa**k**	*bears*
omaškīkō	*Cree (north)*	omaškīkō**k**	*Crees*
omahkahkī	*a frog*	omahkahkī**k**	*frogs*

5. *-īk*

Singular		Plural	
ahsin	*a rock*	ahsin**īk**	*rocks*
sinkop	*a spruce tree*	sinkop**īk**	*spruce trees*

6. *-ak*

Singular		Plural	
animohš	*a dog*	animohš**ak**	*dogs*
mahınkan	*a wolf*	mahınkan**ak**	*wolves*
ihkwēsēns	*a little girl*	ihkwēsēns**ak**	*little girls*
šīhšīp	*a duck*	šīhšīp**ak**	*ducks*

Some animate nouns have no plural suffixes. These are called **mass nouns**. Mass nouns express a quantity that cannot be counted or divided into smaller units. Some examples of mass nouns are:

šōniyā	*money*
mantāmin	*corn*
ahsēmā	*tobacco*
kišīpīkahikan	*face soap*

INANIMATE NOUN PLURAL SUFFIXES

Like animate nouns, inanimate nouns can take different plural suffixes. All inanimate noun plural suffixes end with -*n*, as the following examples show.

1. -*ōn*

Singular		**Plural**	
wāwan	*an egg*	wāwan**ōn**	*eggs*
mihtik	*a stick*	mihtik**ōn**	*sticks*
atōhpowināhk	*a table*	atōhpowināhk**ōn**	*tables*
atāwēwikamik	*a store*	atāwēwikamik**ōn**	*stores*

2. -*īn*

Singular		**Plural**	
wāpikwan	*a flower*	wāpikwan**īn**	*flowers*
sākahikan	*a lake*	sākahikan**īn**	*lakes*
āsokan	*a bridge*	āsokan**īn**	*bridges*

3. -*an*

Singular		**Plural**	
otāpān	*a car*	otāpān**an**	*cars*
wēpahikan	*a broom*	wēpahikan**an**	*brooms*
wāhkāhikan	*a house*	wāhkāhikan**an**	*houses*
tēhsitiyēpiwin	*a chair*	tēhsitiyēpiwin**an**	*chairs*
minihkwācikan	*a cup*	minihkwācikan**an**	*cups*

4. -*n*

Singular		**Plural**	
iškotē	*a fire*	iškotē**n**	*fires*
mīhkana	*a road*	mīhkana**n**	*roads*
sīpi	*a river*	sīpi**n**	*rivers*
ōtēna	*a town/village*	ōtēna**n**	*towns/villages*

For extra practise, see the Chapter 4 Exercises on pages 153–154.

CHAPTER

• • • • • • • • • • •

5

Objectives

- Pre-nouns
- Demonstrative, Interrogative, and Personal Pronouns

Dialogues

1. Awēnēn awē?   *Who is this?*
   Oškinīkīns awē.   *This is a little boy.*
   Awēnēn awē?   *Who is that?*
   Ihkwēsēns awē.   *That is a little girl.*
   Awēnēn awēti?   *Who is that in the distance?*
   Kīsihs awēti.   *That is the sun in the distance.*

2. Wēkonēn owē?   *What is this?*
   Masinahikan owē.   *This is a book.*
   Wēkonēn iwē?   *What is that?*
   Cīmān iwē.   *That is a boat.*
   Wēkonēn iwēti?   *What is that in the distance?*
   Wāhkāhikan iwēti.   *That is a house in the distance.*

3. Ānti kīn?   *Where are you?*
Nīn omā.   *I'm here.*
Ānahpī kīn kā-wīhsiniyan?   *When did you (sg) eat?*
Nōmaya nīn nikī-wīhsin.   *I ate a little while ago.*
Kēkīn na kikī-wīhsin?   *Did you eat also?*
Mīnankē kēnīn nikī-wīhsin.   *Yes, me too I ate.*

Vocabulary

awēnēn	*who?*	wēkonēn	*what?*
ānahpī	*when?*	ānti	*where?*
ānīhšwīn	*why?*	ānīn	*how/what?*
awē	*this* (NA)	owē	*this* (NI)
awē	*that* (NA)	iwē	*that* (NI)
onkowē	*these* (NA)	onowē	*these* (NI)
inkiwē	*those* (NA)	iniwē	*those* (NI)
omā	*here*	imā	*there*
īwiti	*over there*	awēti	*that in the distance*

Pre-nouns

Pre-nouns are placed in front of nouns to add additional information about the noun named. Some pre-verbs used with nouns become pre-nouns. Pre-verbs will be discussed in Chapter 9.

kihci-kōhkōhš	*a **big** pig*
mayaki-anihšināpēk	***strange** Indians*
maci-oškinīkīns	*a **bad** boy*

Pronouns

Pronouns are words used instead of nouns. In English these are words such as *I*, *he*, *we*, *who*, *whose*, *this*, and *that*. For example, instead of saying *the girl*, we could say *she*, or rather than saying, "Pass **the book with the blue cover** to me," we could say, "Please pass **that** to me." Saulteaux has three types of pronouns: demonstrative, interrogative, and personal.

DEMONSTRATIVE PRONOUNS

Demonstrative pronouns are "pointing words": they point to the noun referred to. They agree with the nouns they modify, in gender (*animate and inanimate*), obviation,* and in number (*singular and plural*). Where English uses one word, *this, that, these,* or *those*, Saulteaux has *two sets* of demonstrative pronouns, one for animate nouns (singular and plural) and one for inanimate nouns (singular and plural), as shown in the following table.

	Animate	Inanimate	English translation
Singular	awē	owē	*this*
	awē	iwē	*that*
	awēti	iwēti	*that in the distance*
Plural	onkowē	onowē	*these*
	inkiwē	iniwē	*those*
	inkiwēti	iniwēti	*those in the distance*

Most Saulteaux dialects will collapse the demonstrative pronouns: *awē* to *a, aa,* or *waha*; *owē* to *o, oo*; and *iwē* to *i, ii*. The plural forms are also collapsed: *onkowē* to *onko, okowē, oko*; *onowē* to *ono, onowēn*; *inkiwē* to *inki, ikiwē, iki*; *iniwē* to *ini, iniwēn*. Some dialects will add the animate or inanimate ending to the pronoun and lengthen the final vowel: *inkiwēti* to *inkiwētīk*; *iniwēti* to *iniwētīn*.

Singular Forms

Awē and *awēti* are the singular demonstrative pronouns used when talking about nouns that denote living things, but Saulteaux also has many other nouns that are not living but are classified as being animate.

awē inini	*that/this* man
awēti inini	*that* man *in the distance*
awē otāpānāhk	*that/this* wagon
awēti otāpānāhk	*that* wagon *in the distance*

The examples above show that demonstrative pronouns must agree with the nouns in gender (animate) and number (singular).

---

* Animate and inanimate noun obviation is a distinction made between third persons in a given context. It is used to express relationships to others in the third person, such as *her friend* or *their cousin*. Obviation will be discussed in more detail in Chapter 7 in relation to kinship terms, as well as in chapters discussing verbs.

Owē, iwē, and *iwēti* are the singular demonstrative pronouns used when talking about inanimate nouns.

owē cīmān	*this* boat
iwēti cīmān	*that* boat *in the distance*
owē otēhimin	*this* strawberry
iwēti otēhimin	*that* strawberry *in the distance*

Again, the examples above show that demonstrative pronouns must agree with the nouns in gender (inanimate) and number (singular).

In reference to demonstrative pronouns, word order has an effect on the meaning. When the demonstrative pronoun comes after the noun, the phrase has a different meaning than when it comes before the noun. When the demonstrative pronoun comes before the noun, it is translated as "this one," as in *owē masinahikan* "this book." When the demonstrative pronoun comes after the noun, it is translated as "this is a…," as in *masinahikan owē* "this is a book."

awē mahkwa	*this* bear (animate, singular)
owē cīmān	*this* boat (inanimate, singular)
ihkwē **awē**	*that* is a woman (animate, singular)
wāhkāhikan **iwē**	*that* is a house (inanimate, singular)

Plural Forms

Onkowē, inkiwē, and *inkiwēti* are the plural demonstrative pronouns used when talking about nouns that denote living things (remember Saulteaux has many non-living animate nouns).

inkiwē ininiwak	*those* men (animate, plural)
onkowē ohpwākanak	*these* pipes (animate, plural)

Onowē, iniwē, and *iniwēti* are the plural demonstrative pronouns used when talking about inanimate nouns.

iniwē mahkisinan	*those* shoes (inanimate, plural)
onowē wāpikwanīn	*these* flowers (inanimate, plural)

Remember that the terms *animate* and *inanimate* are genders. Knowing whether a noun is animate or inanimate helps to determine which demonstrative pronoun to use. More on animate and inanimate nouns will be discussed in Chapters 6 and 7.

Other Demonstrative Pronouns

There are other demonstrative pronouns that refer to a specific location (near/far) or direction, such as the following:

omā	*here*
imā	*there*
īwiti	*over there*

Some dialects will pronounce the /ī/ in īwiti with a /ō/ as in ōwiti (especially with pointing lips). These pronouns are used with both animate and inanimate nouns and verbs.

kimiwan omā	*it's raining here*	apin imā	*sit there*
awēti ihkwē īwiti	*that woman over there*	iwē mahkisin imā	*that shoe there*

INTERROGATIVE PRONOUNS

Interrogative pronouns are words that are used to ask supplementary questions. This group of questions asks for information of a certain sort, and in English these sentences often begin with the words *who*, *what*, *where*, *when*, *why*, and *how*. The Saulteaux interrogative pronouns also come at the beginning of the sentence.

awēnēn	*Who?*	wēkonēn	*What?*
ānahpī	*When?*	ānti	*Where?*
ānīhšwīn	*Why?*	ānīn	*How/what?*

In English most of these interrogative pronouns begin with wh- and in Saulteaux most of them begin with *ān-*, so they can be referred to as "WH- questions" or "*ān-* questions." However, unlike in English, the Saulteaux interrogatives also have plurals:

awēnēnak	*who* (pl)	with animate nouns, refers to more than one person
wēkonēnan	*what* (pl)	with animate/inanimate nouns, refers to more than one thing

The following examples contain singular and plural demonstrative and interrogative pronouns.

Wēkonēn owē?	*What is this?*	Wēkonēnan onowē?	*What are these?*
Wēkonēn iwē?	*What is that?*	Wēkonēnan iniwē?	*What are those?*
Awēnēn awē?	*Who is this?*	Awēnēnak onkowē?	*Who are these?*
Awēnēn awē?	*Who is that?*	Awēnēnak inkiwē?	*Who are those?*
Wēkonēn iwēti?	*What is that (in the distance)?*		
Wēkonēnan iniwēti?	*What are those (in the distance)?*		
Awēnēn awēti?	*Who is that (in the distance)?*		
Awēnēnak inkiwēti?	*Who are those (in the distance)?*		

PERSONAL PRONOUNS

The Saulteaux language has seven **personal pronouns**. In contrast, English uses eleven different pronouns: subject pronouns (*I*, *you*, *she/he*, *we*, and *they*) and object pronouns (*me*, *you*, *him/her*, *us*, and *them*). In Saulteaux, the subject of a sentence is represented not with a pronoun but with an affix attached to the verb, as we will see in Chapter 12.

The following abbreviations are used to represent the personal pronouns.

1S	1st person singular	1P	1st person plural (exclusive)
		21	1st person plural (inclusive)
2S	2nd person singular	2P	2nd person plural
3S	3rd person singular	3P	3rd person plural

Note that Saulteaux personal pronouns distinguish between first person plural exclusive and inclusive, abbreviated as 1P and 21, respectively. They also differentiate between "you" (singular) and "you" (plural).

Saulteaux Personal Pronouns			
Person	**Personal pronoun**	**Person**	**Personal pronoun**
1S	nīn – *me*	1P	nīnawint – *us* (ex)
		21	kīnawint – *us* (in)
2S	kīn – *you*	2P	kīnawā – *you people*
3S	wīn – *him/her*	3P	wīnawā – *them*

Nīnawint (1P) means "us excluding the party addressed," and *kīnawint* (21) means "us including the party addressed." This distinction is observed not only in the personal pronouns but in the verbs as well.

Nīnawint nika-anohkīmin.	*Us we will work.* (the person addressed is excluded)
Kīnawint kika-anohkīmin.	*Us we will work.* (the person addressed is excluded)

The personal pronouns such as *you* (singular and plural) and *us* (exclusive and inclusive) have to be explained to non-Saulteaux speakers. The English words *you* and *we* are ambiguous, whereas their use in Saulteaux is much more specific. English uses *you* both when speaking to one person and when speaking to more than one person. Many English speakers have tried to make up for this deficiency by creating *youse*, *you guys*, and *y'all* as plurals for *you*. In Saulteaux, *you* (singular) is expressed by the personal pronoun *kīn* and *you* (plural) is expressed by the personal pronoun *kīnawā*. An English-speaking person who is learning Saulteaux will have to get used to keeping the various meanings of these words separate and distinct. The personal affixes are also different on verbs that express *you* (singular and plural) and *we* (exclusive and inclusive). This will be shown in the following chapters on verbs.

Emphatic Personal Pronouns

Emphatic personal pronouns may be preceded and modified by the particle *kē-* to express emphasis. In English, emphasis is expressed by including the words *too* or *also* with the pronoun, as in: *me too/also, you too/also, him/her too/also.*

Person	Emphatic pronoun	Person	Emphatic pronoun
1S	kēnīn – *me too/also*	1P	kēnīnawint – *us too/also* (ex)
		21	kēkīnawint – *us too/also* (in)
2S	kēkīn – *you too/also*	2P	kēkīnawā – *you people too/also*
3S	kēwīn – *him/her too/also*	3P	kēwīnawā – *them too/also*

Kēkīn na kikī-wīhsin?	*Did **you** eat **also**?*
Kī-išā ōtēnānk **kēwīn**.	*He went to town **also**.*
Nīn **ēhta** nikī-išā imā.	***Only (me)** I went there.*
Kikišiš na **kēkīn**?	*Are **you** hot **also**?*
Kēnīn kayē niwī-anta-anohkī.	***Me too**. I'm going to go to work **also**.*

The particles *kayē* "too/also" and *ēhta* "only" used with an emphatic personal pronoun gives more emphasis to the subject *I*.

For extra practise, see the Chapter 5 Exercises on pages 155–156.

CHAPTER

· · · · · · · · · ·

6

Objectives

- Diminutive nouns
- Locative nouns
- Pejorative nouns
- Compound nouns

Dialogues

1. Ānti ēšāyan?
Atāwēwikamikōnk nitišā.

Where are you going?
I'm going to the store.

2. Ānti kā-išāwāt?
Ōtēnānk kī-išāwak.

Where did they go?
They went to town.

3. Ānti wēntohsēyan?
Sākahikanīnk nitōntohsē.

Where are you coming from?
I come from the lake.

4. Ānti kā-išāyan pihcīnāko?
Ōtēnānk nikī-išā.

Where did you go yesterday?
I went to town.

5. Ānti ēšāt animohšihš?
Wāhkāhikanink išā animohšihš.

Where is the darn dog going?
The darn dog is going to the house.

Vocabulary

ahsin	*rock*	wāwan	*egg*
ahsinīk	*rocks*	wāwanōn	*eggs*
ahsinīns	*little rock*	wāwanōns	*little egg*
āmō	*bee*	otāpān	*car*
āmōns	*little bee*	otāpānēns	*little car*
āmōk	*bees*	otāpānēnsihš	*darn little car*
sīpīnk		*in/on/at/to/by the river(s)*	
tēhsitiyēpiwinink		*in/on/at/to/by the chair*	
nipēwinink		*in/on/at/to/by the bed*	
atāwēwikamikōnk		*in/on/at/to/by the store*	
sākahikanīnk		*in/on/at/to/by the lake*	
kihkinahomākēwikamikōnk		*in/on/at/to/by the school*	

Diminutive Nouns

In Saulteaux you create a **diminutive noun** (to denote that the thing you are talking about is small or little) by attaching a *diminutive suffix* to it. English also has diminutive suffixes, such as *-ling* in "duckling" and *-let* in "piglet." The Saulteaux diminutive suffixes are: *-(y)ēns*, *-īns*, *-ōns*, and *-āns*.

There are rules to follow when attaching the diminutive suffix to a noun, however. The plural suffix of the noun must be known in order to know which diminutive suffix to use. Plural suffixes for animate nouns are *-ak, -yak, -īk, -ōk, -wak, -k*, and plural suffixes for *inanimate* nouns are *-an, -īn, -ōn, -n*.

Rules for attaching diminutive suffixes are as follows:

1. Nouns that take the animate plural suffix *-ak* and the inanimate plural suffix *-an* will take the diminutive suffix *-ēns*:

	Singular	Plural	Diminutive
Animate -ak → -ēns	šīhšīp – *duck*	šīhšīp**ak** – *duck***s**	šīhšīp**ēns** – ***little*** duck
Inanimate -an → -ēns	mahkisin – *shoe*	mahkisin**an** – *shoe***s**	mahkisin**ēns** – ***little*** shoe

Animate nouns that end in *ī* add a *-y-* between the noun and the plural suffix *-ak*, creating the irregular plural suffix *-yak*. These same nouns add *-y-* to the diminutive suffix *-ēns*, creating the irregular diminutive suffix *-yens*, as in the following examples:

pinēhsīyak	*birds*	pinēhsīyēns	***little** bird*
apinōcīyak	*children*	apinōcīyēns	***little** child*

2. Nouns that take the animate plural suffix *-īk* and the inanimate plural suffix *-n* will change the short *-i* to a long *-ī* and become the diminutive suffix *-īns*:

	Singular	Plural	Diminutive
Animate *-īk → -īns*	ahsin – *rock*	ahsin**īk** – *rock**s***	ahsin**īns** – ***little** rock*
Inanimate *-n → -īns*	sīpi – *river*	sīp**īn** – *river**s***	sīp**īns** – ***little** river*

3. Nouns that take the animate plural suffix *-ōk* and the inanimate plural suffix *-ōn* will take the diminutive suffix *-ōns*:

	Singular	Plural	Diminutive
Animate *-ōk → -ōns*	anank – *star*	anank**ōk** – *star**s***	anank**ōns** – ***little** star*
Inanimate *-ōn → -ōns*	wāwan – *egg*	wāwan**ōn** – *egg**s***	wāwan**ōns** – ***little** egg*

4. Nouns that take the animate plural suffix *-k* and the inanimate plural suffix *-n* take the diminutive suffix *-āns*:

	Singular	Plural	Diminutive
Animate *-k → -āns*	okimā – *king/boss*	okimā**k** – *king**s**/boss**es***	okimā**ns** – ***little** king/boss*
Inanimate *-n → -āns*	ōtēna – *town/village*	ōtēna**n** – *town**s**/village**s***	ōtēnā**ns** – ***little** town/village*

There are exceptions to these rules. Some animate nouns that take the plural suffix *-wak* and sometimes *-k* will take different diminutive suffixes than indicated in the rules. There are no rules to these exceptions; they just have to be learned:

	Singular	Plural	Diminutive
Animate -wak → -īns	inini – *man*	inini**wak** – *men*	inin**īns** – **little** *man*
Animate -wak → -ēns	ihkwē – *woman*	ihkwē**wak** – *women*	ihkwē**sēns** – **little** *woman/girl*
Animate -k → -ōns	mahkwa – *bear*	mahk**wak** – *bears*	mahk**ōns** – **little** *bear/cub*
Animate -k → -ōns	āmō – *bee*	āmō**k** – *bees*	ām**ōns** – **little** *bee*

To pluralize diminutive nouns, the plural suffix is attached after the diminutive suffix, as in the following examples. All animate nouns put in the diminutive form will take *-ak* in the plural form, and all inanimate nouns put in the diminutive form will take *-an* in the plural form. The plural suffix is based on the diminutive suffix.

Pl. suffix	Singular form	Diminutive form	Plural form
-an	cīmān – *boat/canoe*	cīmān<u>ēns</u> – <u>*little*</u> *boat/canoe*	cīmān<u>ēns</u>**an** – <u>*little*</u> *boats/canoes*
-ak	ohpwākan – *pipe*	ohpwākan<u>ēns</u> – <u>*little*</u> *pipe*	ohpwākan<u>ēns</u>**ak** – <u>*little*</u> *pipes*
-īk	ahsin – *rock/stone*	ahsin<u>īns</u> – <u>*little*</u> *rock/stone*	ahsin<u>īns</u>**ak** – <u>*little*</u> *rocks/stones*
-īn	sīpi – *river*	sīp<u>īns</u> – <u>*little*</u> *river*	sīp<u>īns</u>**an** – <u>*little*</u> *rivers*
-ōk	anank – *star*	anank<u>ōns</u> – <u>*little*</u> *star*	anank<u>ōns</u>**ak** – <u>*little*</u> *stars*
-ōn	wāwan – *egg*	wāwan<u>ōns</u> – <u>*little*</u> *egg*	wāwan<u>ōns</u>**an** – <u>*little*</u> *eggs*

Locative Nouns

In the Saulteaux language you indicate relative location by attaching a *locative suffix* to a noun. In English this is expressed by prepositions such as *in*, *on*, *at*, *by*, and *to*. The Saulteaux locative suffixes are *-ink*, *-īnk*, *-ōnk*, *-ānk*.

There are rules to follow when attaching the locative suffix to a noun. Similar to diminutives, the plural suffix of the noun must be known in order to know which locative suffix to use.

Plural suffixes for animate nouns are *-ak*, *-yak*, *-īk*, *-ōk*, *-wak*, and *-k*, and plural suffixes for inanimate nouns are *-an*, *-īn*, *-ōn*, and *-n*.

Rules for attaching locative suffixes are as follows:

1. Nouns that take the animate plural suffix *-ak* and the inanimate plural suffix *-an* take the locative suffix *-ink*:

	Singular	Plural	Locative
Animate *-ak → -ink*	tēwēhikan – *drum*	tēwēhikan**ak** – *drums*	tēwēhikan**ink** – *in/on/at/ by/to the drum(s)*
Inanimate *-an → -ink*	cīmān – *boat/canoe*	cīmān**an** – *boats/canoes*	cīmān**ink** – *in/on/at/ by/to the boat(s)/canoe(s)*

2. Nouns that take the animate plural suffix *-īk* and the inanimate plural suffix *-īn* take the locative suffix *-īnk*:

	Singular	Plural	Locative
Animate *-īk → -ink*	ahsin – *rock*	ahsin**īk** – *rocks*	ahsin**īnk** – *in/on/at/by/to the rock(s)*
Inanimate *-īn → -ink*	sīpi – *river*	sīp**īn** – *rivers*	sīp**īnk** – *in/on/at/by/to the river(s)*

3. Nouns that take the animate plural suffix *-ōk* and the inanimate plural suffix *-ōn* take the locative suffix *-ōnk*:

	Singular	Plural	Locative
Animate *-ōk → -ōnk*	anank – *star*	anank**ōk** – *stars*	anank**ōnk** – *in/on/at/by/ to the star(s)*
Inanimate *-ōn → -ōnk*	wāwan – *egg*	wāwan**ōn** – *eggs*	wāwan**ōnk** – *in/on/at/by/ to the egg(s)*

4. Some nouns that take the inanimate plural suffix *-n* will take the locative suffix *-ānk*:

	Singular	Plural	Locative
Inanimate *-n → -ānk*	ōtēna – *town/village*	ōtēna**n** – *towns/villages*	ōtēn**ānk** – *in/on/at/by/to the town(s)/village(s)*

These locative suffixes are never used with people and only rarely used with animals. When adding a locative suffix to a person or an animal, the locative suffix is -*ink*. Besides being translated as *in*, *on*, *at*, *by*, or *to*, it can be translated as *like*. For example, *kōhkōhšink* means "pig-like," and *animohšink* means "dog-like."

kōhkōhš**ink** iši-ayā	*she/he is/acts like a pig*
animohš**ink** išinākoši	*she/he looks like a dog*
animohš**ink** iši-ayā	*she/he is/acts like a dog*

The following example asks the question "where?" and gives the answer using a locative noun.

Q: ānti ēhtēk sīwihtākan?   Where is the salt?
    where it sits   salt

A: akōcikan**ink**   ahtē.   *It is (sitting) in the cupboard.*
    in/on/at/by/to the cupboard   it is sitting

Pejorative Nouns

In the Saulteaux language, when one is showing anger or disgust, a pejorative suffix may be attached to a noun to indicate this. The suffix -*ihš* is used after a consonant and -*wihš* is used after a vowel. English uses a word such as *darn*. This suffix is used with both common nouns and proper nouns, as the examples below indicate.

Oškinīkīns**ihš** niniškihik.	***Darn*** *little boy, gets me mad.*
inini**wihš**	***darn*** *man*
John**ihš**	***darn*** *John*
Anna**wihš**	***darn*** *Anna*
animohš**ihš**	***darn*** *dog*

To make a diminutive noun a pejorative noun, the diminutive suffix comes after the noun and the perjorative suffix is then attached after the diminutive suffix.

Pej. suffix	Singular form	Diminutive form	Pejorative form
-*ihš*	animohš – *dog*	anim**ōns** – ***little*** *dog*	animōns**ihš** – ***darn*** *little dog*
-*ihš*	otāpān – *car*	otāpān**ēns** – ***little*** *car*	otāpānēns**ihš** – ***darn*** *little car*

To pluralize these nouns, the plural suffix is attached at the end of the noun, so the other suffixes, whatever type (diminutive or pejorative; locatives do not have a plural suffix, etc.), are attached before the plural suffix. For example:

kōhkōhšēnsihšak				*darn little pigs*
kōhkōhš +	-ēns +	-ihš +	-ak	
NA	DIM. SF	PEJ. SF	PL. ANIMATE SF	

cīmānēnsihšan				*darn little boats*
cīmān +	-ēns +	-ihš +	-an	
NA	DIM. SF	PEJ. SF	PL. INANIMATE SF	

Compound Nouns

In Saulteaux, you can create a **compound noun** (or a new noun) by joining two nouns together with a hyphen. In some cases, a verb and a noun together will make a compound.

mihtik(o) + wanīhikan = mihtiko-wanīhikan   *wooden trap*
tree/stick   *trap*

iškotē(w) + otāpān = iškotēw-otāpān   *train* (lit., *fire vehicle*)
fire   *vehicle*

A vowel is usually added when the first word ends in a consonant, as in the first example (o), and the consonant *w* is always added when the first word ends in a vowel, as in the second example. Some compounds are made with only the stem of the word, as in *wāpi-mahkwa* "white bear," which consists of the V-AI *wāpiškisi* "she/he is white" and the noun *mahkwa* "bear." The verb stem *wāpi-* is used, or the verb root can also be used, as in *wāpiški-mahkwa* "white bear."

BUILDING SUFFIX

The words for particular buildings are created by attaching the suffix *-wikamik* to the noun or verb that describes what the building is used for, as in the following examples:

wīhsini	+	**wikamik**	=	wīhsinīwikamik
V		SUFFIX		NI (INANIMATE)
she/he is eating		*building*	=	*restaurant* (lit., *eating building*)

āhkosi	+	**wikamik**	=	āhkosīwikamik
she/he is sick		*building*	=	*hospital* (lit., *sick building*)

otamino	+	**wikamik**	=	otaminōwikamik
she/he is playing		*building*	=	*recreation hall* (lit., *playing building*)

atāwē	+	**wikamik**	=	atāwēwikamik
she/he buys		*building*	=	*store* (lit., *buying building*)

šōniyā	+	**wikamik**	=	šōniyāwikamik
money		*building*	=	*bank* (lit., *money building*)

kihkinahomākē	+	**wikamik**	=	kihkinahomākēwikamik
she/he is teaching		*building*	=	*school* (lit., *teaching building*)

kihci-	+	kihkēntāhso	+ **wikamik**	=	kihci-kihkēntāhsōwikamik
great		*she/he has knowledge*	*building*	=	*university* (lit., *great knowledge building*)

When the building suffix is attached to a noun or verb that ends in a short vowel, the vowel becomes long as in the first three examples above.

For extra practise, see the Chapter 6 Exercises on pages 157–158.

CHAPTER

•   •   •   •   •   •   •   •   •   •

7

Objectives

- Possessive nouns—animate and inanimate
- Dependent nouns—kinship and anatomical terms

Dialogues

1. Awēnēn kimihšōmihš? *Who is your grandfather?*
    John nimihšōmihš. *John is my grandfather.*

2. Ānti ēyāt kimāmā? *Where is your mother at?*
    Ayapi nimāmā. *My mother is at home.*

3. Awēnēn kipāpā? *Who is your father?*
    Pat nipāpā. *Pat is my father.*

4. Kōhkō na ayapi? *Is your grandmother at home?*
    Mīnankē nōhko ayapi. *Yes, my grandmother is home.*

5. Ānīn ēšinihkāsot kihsayē? *What is your older brother's name?*
    George išinihkāso nihsayē. *My older brother's name is George.*

6. Ānīn ēšinihkāsot kimihsē? *What is your older sister's name?*
    Norinne išinihkāso nimihsē. *My older sister's name is Norinne.*

Vocabulary

nimāmā	*my mother*	nipāpā	*my father*
nōhkō	*my grandmother*	nimihšōmihš	*my grandfather*
nikosihsak	*my sons*	nitānihs	*my daughter*
nihsayē	*my older brother*	nimihsē	*my older sister*
ninīkīkōk	*my parents*	nisīmēns	*my younger sister*
ninōsihs	*my grandchild*	ninōhsēyēns	*my little grandchild*
nimasinahikan	*my book*	nimasinahikanan	*my books*
nipōsīnsim	*my cat*	nipōsīnsimak	*my cats*
kikōhkōhšimiwāk	*your pigs*	okōhkōhšimiwān	*their pig*
nitahsēmā	*my tobacco*	kišōniyām	*your money*
nīyaw	*my body*	nikanakīnk	*my face*
ninincīn	*my hands*	ninisīkinincān	*my finger*
nitēh	*my heart*	nimihsat	*my stomach*

Possessive Nouns

In the Saulteaux language, *possessive nouns* are nouns that are possessed or owned by someone or something. English uses possessive pronouns such as *my, your, his/her, our,* and *their.* The following abbreviations are used to represent the persons used with possessive nouns in Saulteaux.

1s	1st person singular – *my*	1P	1st person plural (exclusive) – *our*
		21	1st person plural (inclusive) – *our*
2s	2nd person singular – *your*	2P	2nd person plural – *your*
3s	3rd person singular – *his/her*	3P	3rd person plural – *their*
3's	3rd person singular obviative – *his/her*	3'P	3rd person plural obviative – *his/her*

Saulteaux shows possession by attaching possessive affixes to the noun. The possessive affixes are *both* prefixes and suffixes. The possessive prefixes *ni-, ki-,* and *o-* are used with body parts and kinship terms as well as other nouns. Inanimate nouns with these prefixes can be singular (no suffix) or plural (add the plural suffix).

nimasinahikan	**my** book	**ni**masinahikan**an**	**my** books
kimasinahikan	**your** book	**ki**masinahikan**an**	**your** books
omasinahikan	**his/her** book	**o**masinahikan**an**	**his/her** books

In the examples above, *ni-* (my) is the 1st person singular prefix indicating that the book belongs to me, and *ki-* (your) is the 2nd person singular prefix indicating it belongs to you. English uses *'s* after nouns to show 3rd person possession, as in *your father's boat*, where the first noun (*your father*) possesses the second noun (*boat*). Saulteaux uses *o-* for the 3rd person possessor:

kipāpā **ocīmān**   *your father's boat* (lit., *your father, his boat*)

ki-	+	pāpā	o-	+	cīmān
your		*father*	*his*		*boat*

Many animate nouns also have the possessive suffixes *-im*, *-ōm*, or *-m*, as in **nipōsīnsim** "my cat," but not all animate nouns will take these suffixes. This doesn't follow a rule but must be memorized. Nouns that end in *-n* do not take this possessive suffix.

pōsīns	*a cat*	**ni**pōsīn**sim**	*my cat*
kīhsohkān	*a clock*	**ni**kīhsohkān	*my clock*

When nouns begin with a vowel, a connector *-t-* is inserted between the person possessive and the noun. In the Saulteaux writing system two vowels are never together.

ahkihk   *a pail*   ni**t**ahkihk**ōm**   *my pail*

If the noun begins in a short *o*, the vowel then becomes long *ō* when the connector *-t-* is attached.

ohpwākan   *a pipe*   ni**tō**hpwākan   *my pipe*

Possessive nouns are pluralized by attaching the plural suffixes to the noun. Inanimate nouns take plural suffixes that end in *-n*, and animate nouns take plural suffixes that end in *-k*.

nimasinahikan	*my book*	nimasinahikan**an**	*my books*
nipōsīn**sim**	*my cat*	nipōsīnsim**ak**	*my cats*

ANIMATE NOUN FORMS

Animate nouns that end in *-n* would take the possessive affixes, with the exception of *-im*, *-ōm* or *-m*. The possessive suffix *-im* precedes the personal and plural suffix. The symbols *-n → -h* in the following table indicate that the *-n* is changed to *-h* in the plural form.

Person	poss. pref. / noun / (poss. suf.) / pers. suf. /{pl. suf.}	Translation
1S	ni- / noun / (-im) / {-ak}	*my*
2S	ki- / noun / (-im) / {-ak}	*your*
3S	o- / noun / (-im) / -an {-n → -h}	*his/her*
3'S	o- / noun / (-im) / -iniwan {-n → -h}	*his/her* (obviative)
1P	ni- / noun / (-im) / -inān {-ik}	*our* (ex)
21	ki- / noun / (-im) / -inān {-ik}	*our* (in)
2P	ki- / noun / (-im) / -iwā {-k}	*your*
3P	o- / noun / (-im) / -iwān {-n → -h}	*their*
3'P	o- / noun / (-im) / -iniwān {-n → -h}	*his/her* (obviative)

The following is an example of an animate noun in the possessive forms using the suffix *-im* forms.

kōhkōhš – *pig*

	Singular		*Plural*	
1S	ni**kōhkōhšim** (*-an*)	***my*** pig	ni**kōhkōhšimak**	*my pigs*
2S	ki**kōhkōhšim** (*-an*)	***your*** pig	ki**kōhkōhšimak**	*your pigs*
3S	o**kōhkōhšiman**	***his/her*** pig	o**kōhkōhšimah**	*his/her pigs*
3'S	o**kōhkōhšiminiwān**	***his/her*** pig	o**kōhkōhšiminiwāh**	*his/her pigs*
1P	ni**kōhkōhšiminān** (*-in*)	***our*** pig (ex)	ni**kōhkōhšiminānik**	*our pigs* (ex)
21	ki**kōhkōhšiminān** (*-in*)	***our*** pig (in)	ki**kōhkōhšiminānik**	*our pigs* (in)
2P	ki**kōhkōhšimiwā** (*-n*)	***your*** pig	ki**kōhkōhšimiwāk**	*your pigs*
3P	o**kōhkōhšimiwān**	***their*** pig	o**kōhkōhšimiwāh**	*their pigs*
3'P	o**kōhkōhšiminiwān**	***his/her*** pig	o**kōhkōhšiminiwāh**	*his/her pigs*

The 1st person and 2nd person obviative suffixes are in parentheses and italicized. When something animate belongs to a 3rd person, it is *always* in the obviative form. The possessive animate noun forms can also take the diminutive, locative, and pejorative suffixes, as in *nikōhkōhšimihš* "my darn pig." The locative suffix for animate singular forms is *-ink* and for plural forms is *-ihkānk*:

nikōhkōhšim**ink**   *in/on/at/by/to my pig*   nikōhkōhšim**ihkānk**   *in/on/at/by/to my pigs*

ANIMATE NOUN OBVIATION

Obviation is a distinction made between third persons in a given context. When two 3rd persons appear in a phrase or sentence, one is obviative and grammatically linked to a more prominent 3rd person. Let's look at the following example:

ihkwē opōsīns**an**	*the woman's cat* (*cat* is singular obviative)
ihkwē opōsīns**ah**	*the woman's cats* (*cats* is plural obviative)

An animate noun is also obviative when it has a 3rd person possessor that begins with *o-* and must take an obviative suffix (*-an, -wan, -yan, -ōn, -in*).

okosihs**an**	*his son*
okōhkōhšim**an**	*his pig*
omōns**ōn**	*his moose*

These forms also distinguish between obviative singular and obviative plural, but only in the 1st and 2nd persons, as the following examples indicate.

1s	nikōhkōhš*im*a**n**	*my pig*	obviative singular
	nikōhkōhš*im*a**h**	*my pigs*	obviative plural
2s	kikōhkōhš*im*a**n**	*your pig*	obviative singular
	kikōhkōhš*im*a**h**	*your pigs*	obviative plural
1P	nikōhkōhš*im*inān**in**	*our pig*	obviative singular (ex)
	nikōhkōhš*im*inān**ih**	*our pigs*	obviative plural (ex)
21	kikōhkōhš*im*inān**in**	*our pig*	obviative singular (in)
	kikōhkōhš*im*inān**ih**	*our pigs*	obviative plural (in)
2P	kikōhkōhš*im*iw**ān**	*your pig*	obviative singular
	kikōhkōhš*im*iw**āh**	*your pigs*	obviative plural

Remember, animate nouns can be obviative or non-obviative, depending on the context. For example, *my tobacco* is not in the obviative form when it is the direct object of a sentence with a 1st or 2nd person subject (e.g., **I** *offered my tobacco*), but it takes the obviative form if it is the direct object of a third person subject (e.g., **He** *offered his tobacco*).

nitahsēmā	*my tobacco*	
nitahsēmān	*my tobacco*	obviative
kišōniyām	*your money*	
kišōniyāman	*your money*	obviative
ošōniyāman	*his money*	obviative
otahsēmānsah	*his cigarettes*	obviative

The following sentences contain animate possessive nouns:

Ānti nitahsēmā?	*Where is my tobacco?*
Ānti ēpit nitahsēmā?	*Where is my tobacco sitting?*
Kikī-otāhpinimān na kipāpā ošōniyāman?	*Did you take your father's money?* (The money is obviative because *your father* is in third person.)
Mīnankē nikī-otāhpinimān ošōniyāman.	*Yes, I took his money.* (The money is obviative, because *his* is in third person.)
Kikī-mihkawā na nitōhpwākan?	*Did you find my pipe?*

ANIMATE OBVIATIVE DEMONSTRATIVE FORMS

The demonstrative pronouns *onowē* and *iniwē*, which are used to mean "these" and "those" when used with inanimate nouns, are the **animate obviative forms** that must be used whenever the demonstrative pronouns refer to an animate obviative noun. The **animate obviative demonstrative pronouns** are the same in the singular and plural, and they are *identical* to the inanimate plural forms used with demonstrative pronouns in chapter 5.

An animate noun is also *obviative* when it is the direct object of a verb that has a 3rd person subject.

John okī-mihkawān **onowē** kīhsohkānēnsan.	*John found **this** watch.*
John okī-mihkawāh **ono** kīhsohkānēnsah.	*John found **these** watches.*
Mary owāpamān **iniwē** animohšan.	*Mary sees **that** dog.*
Mary owāpamāh **ini** animohšah.	*Mary sees **those** dogs.*

INANIMATE NOUN FORMS

The following table lists the possessive affixes for inanimate nouns. The plural suffixes, shown in brackets { }, are attached to the end of the noun form. Once again, "exclusive" means that the one spoken to (the addressee) is excluded, and "inclusive" means that the addressee is included. The 3's and 3'ᴘ take the same possessive prefix and suffix. (These forms went through a morphological process called **syncretism**, where one form stops being used and is replaced by the other.)

Inanimate Noun Forms		
Person	**poss. pref. / noun / pers. suf. / {pl. suf.}**	**Translation**
1S	ni- / noun / {-an}	*my*
2S	ki- / noun / {-an}	*your*
3S	o- / noun / {-an}	*his/her*
3'S	o- / noun / -ini {-wan}	*his/her* (obviative)
1P	ni- / noun / -inān {-in}	*our* (ex)
21	ki- / noun / -inān {-in}	*our* (in)
2P	ki- / noun / -iwā {-n}	*your*
3P	o- / noun / -iwā {-n}	*their*
3'P	o- / noun / -ini {-wan}	*his/her* (obviative)

Here is an example of the various possessive forms for an inanimate noun:

cīmān – *boat*

1S	nicīmān (-an)	*my boat(s)*
2S	kicīmān (-an)	*your boat(s)*
3S	ocīmān (-an)	*his/her boat(s)*
3'S	ocīmānini (-wan)	*his/her _____'s boat(s)*
1P	nicīmāninān (-in)	*our boat(s)* (ex)
21	kicīmāninān (-in)	*our boat(s)* (in)
2P	kicīmāniwā (-n)	*your boat(s)*
3P	ocīmāniwā (-n)	*their boat(s)*
3'P	ocīmānini (-wan)	*his/her _____s' boat(s)*

The possessive noun forms can also take other nouns suffixes, as in the pejorative *nicīmānihš* "my **darn** boat" or with the following locatives:

1S	nicīmān**ink**	***in/on/at/by/to*** *my boat*
2S	kicīmān**ink**	***in/on/at/by/to*** *your boat*
3S	ocīmān**ink**	***in/on/at/by/to*** *his/her boat*
3'S	ocīmān**inīnk**	***in/on/at/by/to*** *his/her _____'s boat*
1P	nicīmān**inānk**	***in/on/at/by/to*** *our boat* (ex)
21	kicīmān**inānk**	***in/on/at/by/to*** *our boat* (in)
2P	kicīmān**iwānk**	***in/on/at/by/to*** *your boat*
3P	ocīmān**iwānk**	***in/on/at/by/to*** *their boat*
3'P	ocīmān**inīnk**	***in/on/at/by/to*** *his/her _____s' boat*

When an inanimate noun is possessed by a 3rd person and it is the direct object of a verb in the 3rd person, it is obviative.

Okī-otāpinān owīhahkwān.	*He took his (own) hat.*
Okī-otāpinān owīhahkwān**ini**.	*He took his (**someone else's**) hat.*
Okī-pīhkošitōn otōtāpān.	*He wrecked his (own) car.*
Okī-pīhkošitōn otōtāpān**ini**.	*He wrecked his (**someone else's**) car.*

Here are some sentences containing inanimate possessive nouns:

Ānti nimasinahikan?	*Where is my book?*
Ānti ēhtēkin kimasinahikanan?	*Where are your books sitting?*
Kikī-mihkānan na kimahkisinan?	*Did you find your shoes?*
Kāwīn nikī-mihkansīnan nimahkisinan.	*I didn't find my shoes.*
Awēnēn kā-otāhpinank niwīhahkwān?	*Who took my cap?*
John okī-otāhpinān kiwīhahkwān.	*John took your cap.*
Kikī-mihkān na kipāpā owīhahkwān?	*Did you find your father's cap?*

Inanimate nouns do not take a possessive suffix (*-im, -om, -m*), and the 1st and 2nd persons do not take an obviative suffix like the animate nouns do. The following are examples of possessed animate and inanimate nouns.

Animate nouns		*Inanimate nouns*	
nit**ē**w**ē**hikan	*my **drum***	ni**masinahikan**	*my **book***
ot**ē**w**ē**hikanan	*his **drum***	o**masinahikan**	*his **book***
nit**ē**w**ē**hikaninānīk	*our **drums***	ni**masinahikan**inānīn	*our **books***

Dependent Nouns

We have already seen several types of nouns: pronouns, diminutives, locatives, pejoratives, and possessives. Another type of noun in the Saulteaux language is **dependent nouns**. A dependent noun is a form of possessive, but the existence of a dependent noun is dependent upon the existence of the owner. All kinship terms (son, daughter, father, etc.) and anatomical terms (foot, head, heart, etc.) are dependent nouns in Saulteaux because these nouns are always possessed *by someone*; there is no such thing as a son who isn't someone's son or a hand that isn't someone's hand. A dependent noun is a possessive noun.

Along with these are words like *pet*,* whose form changes if the owner is not mentioned. For an example, let's begin with the word for *pet* when the owner corresponds to one of the seven personal pronouns.

Possessive Dependent Noun (tay – *pet*)				
Possessor	**Singular**	**Plural**	**Obviative singular**	**Obviative plural**
1s *my*	nitay	nitayak	nitayan	nitayah
2s *your*	kitay	kitayak	kitayan	kitayah
3s *his/her*	otayan	otayak	otayan	otayah
1P *our* (ex)	nitayinān	nitayinānīk	nitayinānīn	nitayinānih
21 *our* (in)	kitayinān	kitayinānīk	kitayinānīn	kitayinānih
2P *your*	kitayiwā	kitayiwāk	kitayiwān	kitayiwāh
3P *their*	otayiwān	otayiwāh	otayiwān	otayiwāh

As with possessive nouns, the dependent noun forms begin with personal prefixes *ni(t)-*, *ki(t)-*, and *o(t)-* (the *t* is added before nouns that begin in vowels). When the personal pronoun ends in *wint*, as in *ninawint* and *kinawint*, the possessive noun form contains the suffix *-inan*. When the personal pronoun ends in the suffix *-wā*, as in *kīnawā* and *wīnawā*, the possessive noun form contains the suffix *-iwā*.

Animate Dependent Noun			
Person		**Singular**	**Plural**
0	unspecified	apinōcī – *child*	apinōcī**yak** – *children*
1s	nīn – *my*	nitapinōcīhim – *my child*	nitapinōcīhim**ak** – *my children*
2s	kīn – *your*	kitapinōcīhim – *your child*	kitapinōcīhim**ak** – *your children*
3s	wīn – *his/her*	otapinōcīhiman – *his/her child*	otapinōcīhim**ah** – *his/her children*
1P	nīnawint – *our* (ex)	nitapinōcīhiminān – *our child*	nitapinōcīhiminān**ik** – *our children*
21	kīnawint – *our* (in)	kitapinōcīhiminān – *our child*	kitapinōcīhiminān**ik** – *our children*
2P	kīnawā – *your*	kitapinōcīhimiwā – *your child*	kitapinōcīhimiwā**k** – *your children*
3P	wīnawā – *their*	otapinōcīhimiwān – *their child*	otapinōcīhimiwā**h** – *their children*

Note that this animate noun also takes the possessive suffix *-(h)im* (the *h* separates the two vowels and is not pronounced).

---

* Traditionally, the word *tay* referred to a pet horse or pet dog, as these were the only pets the Saulteaux community would have had. Now, *tay* can mean pets of any kind.

The **vocative** is used to denote the person or persons addressed. The vocative plural suffix is
-itok and is used only when addressing people, not when speaking about them.

apinōcī**hitok**	*children!*
nimihšōmih**šitok**	*my grandfathers!*

KINSHIP TERMS

Nitinawēmākanak – *my relatives/family*

nitinawēmākan (-ak)	*my relative(s)*
nitānkōpicikan (-ak)	*my great-grandparent(s)*
nimihšōmihš (-ak)	*my grandfather(s)*
nōhkōmihš (-ak)	*my grandmother(s)*
ninīkīk (-ōk)	*my parent(s)*

Immediate Family

ninīcānihš (-ak)	*my child(ren)*
nikosihs (-ak)	*my son(s)*
nitānihs (-ak)	*my daughter(s)*
nipēpēm (-ak)	*my baby(ies)*
ninōsihs (-ak)	*my grandchild(ren)*
ninōhsēyēns (-ak)	*my little grandchild(ren)*
nitānkōpicikan (-ak)	*my great-grandchild(ren)*
nitānkwē (-yak)	*my sister(s)-in-law or brother's spouse (brothers' spouses)*
nīhtā (-yak)	*my brother(s)-in-law or sister's spouse (sisters' spouses)*

Paternal (Father's) Side

nōhs (-ak)	*my father(s)*
nipāpā (-yak)	*my father(s) (pāpā is an anglicized term)*
nimihšōmē (-yak)	*my uncle(s)*
nitōsihs (-ak)	*my aunt(s) or uncle's wife (uncles' wives)*
nišikohš (-ak)	*my aunt(s) or father's sister(s)*
nišihšē (-yak)	*my uncle(s) or aunt's husband (aunts' husbands)*
nitōhsim (-ak)	*my nephew(s)*
nitōhšimihkwēm (-ak)	*my niece(s)*

Maternal (Mother's) Side

nikā (-yak)	*my mother(s)*
nimāmā (-yak)	*my mother(s) (māmā is an anglicized term)*
ninōhsē (-yak)	*my aunt(s)*
nimāmāyēns (-ak)	*my aunt(s) (māmāyēns "little mother" is an anglicized term)*
nišihšē (-yak)	*my uncle(s) or mother's brother(s)*

nišikohš (-ak)	*my aunt(s) or uncle's wife (uncles' wives)*
ninkwan (-ak)	*my nephew(s)*
nitōhšimihkwēm (-ak)	*my niece(s)*

Extended Family

nīhtāwihš (-ak)	*my male cross cousin(s)*
nitawēmā (-k)	*my female cross cousin(s)*
nīhtā (-yak)	*my male cousin(s) (male speaking)*
nitānkwē (-yak)	*my female cousin(s) (female speaking)*
nitahkiwēnsīhim (-ak)	*my husband(s)*
nimintimōhēhim (-ak)	*my wife (wives)*
niwīcīwākan (-ak)	*my partner(s)*
nitintāwā (-k)	*my in-law(s)*
nišihšē (-yak)	*my father(s)-in-law*
nišikohš (-ak)	*my mother(s)-in-law*
nīnim (-ak)	*my brother(s)-in-law*
nitānkwē (-yak)	*my sister(s)-in-law*
nininkwan (-ak)	*my son(s)-in-law*
nihsimihs (-ak)	*my daughter(s)-in-law*

Others

nikwīmē (-wak)	*my namesake(s)*
nīhcī (-yak)	*my brother(s) or brethren*
nīnimōns (-ak)	*my sweetheart(s)*
nitōtēm (-ak)	*my friend(s)*

The kinship terms can be put into the nine person forms, and the noun forms begin with a personal prefixes, *ni-* (1st persons), *ki-* (2nd persons) and *o-* (3rd persons). The plural forms also take plural suffixes, as shown in the kinship paradigms in the following examples.

Kinship Terms Ending in Vowels		
1s	**ni**hsayē (-yak)	**my** older brother(s)
2s	**ki**hsayē (-yak)	**your** older brother(s)
3s	**o**hsayē*y***an** (-n → **-h**)	**his/her** older brother(s)
3's	**o**hsayē*y***ini** (-h)	**his/her** _____'s older brother(s)
1P	**ni**hsayē*y***inān** (-ik)	**our** (ex) older brother(s)
21	**ki**hsayē*y***inān** (-ik)	**our** (in) older brother(s)
2P	**ki**hsayē*y***iwā** (-k)	**your** older brother(s)
3P	**o**hsayē*y***iwān** (-n → **-h**)	**their** older brother(s)
3'P	**o**hsayē*y***iwānīn** (-n → **-h**)	**his/her** _____s' older brother(s)

Kinship Terms Ending in Consonants		
1s	**ni**tānihs (-ak)	**my** daughter(s)
2s	**ki**tānihs (-ak)	**your** daughter(s)
3s	**o**tānihs**an** (-n → **-h**)	**his/her** daughter(s)
3's	**o**tānihsi**wāni** (-h)	**his/her** _____'s daughter(s)
1P	**ni**tānihsi**nān** (-ik)	**our** (ex) daughter(s)
21	**ki**tānihsi**nān** (-ik)	**our** (in) daughter(s)
2P	**ki**tānihsi**wā** (-k)	**your** daughter(s)
3P	**o**tānihsi**wān** (-n → **-h**)	**their** daughter(s)
3'P	**o**tānihsi**wānīn** (-n → **-h**)	**his/her** _____s' daughter(s)

As with the other animate nouns, the dependent/possessive nouns also take singular and plural obviative suffixes. When a dependent noun is *obviative singular* in the 1st and 2nd person singular, add *-an.*

1s	nitānihs	*my daughter*	1s	nitānihs**an**	*my daughter*
2s	kitānihs	*your daughter*	2s	kitānihs**an**	*your daughter*

When a dependent noun is *obviative plural* in the 1st and 2nd person singular, change the *k* to *h.*

1s	nitānihsa**k**	*my daughters*	1s	nitānihsa**h**	*my daughters*
2s	kitānihsa**k**	*your daughers*	2s	kitānihsa**h**	*your daughters*

When a dependent noun is *obviative singular* in the 1st and 2nd persons plural, add *-in/-n.*

1P	nitānihsinān	*our (ex) daughter*	1P	nitānihsinān**in**	*our (ex) daughter*
21	kitānihsinān	*our (in) daughter*	21	kitānihsinān**in**	*our (in) daughter*
2P	kitānihsiwā	*your daughter*	2P	kitānihsiwā**n**	your daughter

When a dependent noun is *obviative plural* in the 1st and 2nd persons plural, change the *k* to *h.*

1P	nitānihsināni**k**	*our (ex) daughters*	1P	nitānihsināni**h**	*our (ex) daughters*
21	kitānihsināni**k**	*our (in) daughters*	21	kitānihsināni**h**	*our (in) daughters*
2P	kitānihsiwā**k**	*your daughters*	2P	kitānishiwā**h**	*your daughters*

ANATOMICAL TERMS

Anatomical terms are dependent nouns because they depend on the possessor (in Saulteaux, you can't have a head or an arm that doesn't belong to someone). As with the kinship terms above, the anatomical terms will begin with a personal prefix and will also take plural suffixes as shown below.

nīyaw	*my body*	nitatikwākan	*my spine*
nikanakīnk	*my face*	nicīštatēyāpīn	*my muscles*
ništikwān	*my head*	nihpihkwan	*my back*
niwīnitip	*my brain*	nišīkan	*my lower back*
niwīnisihsan	*my hair*	nihkāt (-an)	*my leg(s)*
niškahtik	*my forehead*	nipwām (-an)	*my thigh(s)*
niškīnsik (-ōn)	*my eye(s)*	nikihtik (-ōn)	*my knee(s)*
nimisāpiwin (-an)	*my eyebrow(s)*	ninān (-an)	*my calf (calves)*
nimisāpiwinānan	*my eyelashes*	nihkokwan (-an)	*my shin(s)*
nicān	*my nose*	nisit (-an)	*my foot (feet)*
nihsankwan (-an)	*my cheek(s)*	nitōntan (-an)	*my heel(s)*
nitōn	*my mouth*	ninisīkisitān (-an)	*my toe(s)*
nitōnēns (-an)	*my lip(s)*	ninakākositānan	*my soles of my feet*
nitēnaniw	*my tongue*	ninakišīn	*my intestines*
niwīpitan (-an)	*my tooth (teeth)*	nihkon	*my liver*
nitāmikan	*my chin*	nihpan (-an)	*my lung(s)*
nitawak (-an)	*my ear(s)*	nitōhkošan	*my kidneys*
nihkwēkan	*my neck*	niwīškway	*my bladder*
ninihk (-an)	*my arm(s)*	niškatay	*my skin*
nitinimākan (-an)	*my shoulder(s)*	nitiskwēyāpīn	*my veins*
nihkāhkikan	*my chest*	nimiskwīm	*my blood*
nitēh	*my heart*	nipikayan	*my ribs*
nitōtōhšimah	*my breasts*	nihtihšīns	*my navel*
nimihsat	*my stomach*	ninōnkan (-an)	*my hip(s)*
nitōskwan (-an)	*my elbow(s)*	nitīh	*my rear*
nininc (-īn)	*my hand(s)*	niwīnin	*my fat*
ninisīkinincān (-an)	*my finger(s)*	nihkan (-an)	*my bone(s)*
niškāns (-īh)	*my fingernail(s)*	cīpayikanān	*skeleton*
ninincīns (-an)	*my thumb(s)*	ohkanan	*bones*

The pre-noun *manki-* "big/huge" can be added to anatomical terms to qualify the noun. Only *manki-* is used with anatomical terms; *kihci-* "big/great/huge" is never used.

manki-	+	-štikwān	=	mankištikwān *(big/huge head)*
PRE-NOUN		NOUN STEM		NOUN
manki-	+	-tōn	=	mankitōn *(big mouth)*
manki-	+	-cān	=	mankicān *(big nose)*

For extra practise, see the Chapter 7 Exercises on pages 159–160.

CHAPTER

··········

8

Objectives

- Introduction to verbs
- Verb mode, tense, aspect
- Conjugating verbs

Dialogues

1. Ānīn ēšiwēpahk nōnkom?
   Wāhsēyā nōnkom.

   How is the weather today?
   It is sunny today.

2. Wēkonēn wāpantaman?
   Niwāpantān otāpān.

   What do you see?
   I see a car.

3. Wēkonēn nōntaman?
   Ninōntawā pinēhsī.

   What do you hear?
   I hear a bird.

4. Ānahpī kē-mawatihšiwēyan?
   Nika-mawatihšiwē nīšo-kīšikahk.

   When will you visit?
   I will visit on Tuesday.

Vocabulary

Cīhkēntam.   *She/he is happy.*
Kān cīhkēntansī.   *She/he is not happy.*
Pimohsē.   *She/he is walking.*

Kēko pimohsēhkēn.	*(You) don't walk.*
Wāhsēyā.	*It is sunny.*
Kān wāhsēyāhsinōn.	*It's not sunny.*
Tipihkat.	*It is night.*
Kān tipihkahsinōn.	*It is not night.*
Wāpam.	*(You) see him/her/it.*
Kēko wāpamhkēn.	*(You) don't see him/her/it.*
Nōntaw.	*(You) hear him/her/it.*
Kān ninōntawāhsī.	*I don't hear him/her/it.*
Wāpantan.	*(You) see it.*
Kān niwāpantānsīn.	*I don't see it.*
Nōntan.	*(You) hear it.*
Kēko nōntankēn.	*(You) don't hear it.*

Introduction to Verbs

A **verb** is a part of speech that describes an action, state, or event. In many languages verbs have different forms for tense, voice, and mood. We use the word class *verb*—along with other word classes in Saulteaux, including nouns, pronouns, particles, and pre-verbs—when we are talking about sentence structure.*

There are various types and modes of a verb. In the Saulteaux language the verb is the main part of the sentence/phrase that denotes action. There are four basic forms that a verb might take: *inanimate intransitive* (V-II), *animate intransitive* (V-AI), *transitive animate* (V-TA), and *transitive inanimate* (V-TI).

Animacy refers to living and non-living things, while **transitivity** refers to whether there is a transfer of the action onto another object or not. Compare these examples of the four types of verbs in English:

V-II:	Wāhsēyā.	*It is sunny.*	weather word
	Tipihkat.	*It is night.*	division of day
V-AI:	Cīhkēntam.	*She/he is happy.*	state verb
	Pimohsē.	*She/he is walking.*	action verb
V-TA:	Wāpam.	*(You) see him/her/it.*	animate subject transfers action to an animate object
	Nōntaw.	*(You) hear him/her/it.*	

---

* While we use the term **verb** when talking about sentence structure, there is a related concept—*predicate*—which is used when examining the *relationships* among the words of a sentence. That is, we talk about the predicate in terms of its grammatical relations with the subject and object. For simplicity of terminology, in this introductory textbook we use only the term *verb* when discussing grammatical relationships. However, advanced students of Saulteaux will want to clearly distinguish between the two concepts.

| V-TI: | Wāpantan. | *(You) see it.* | animate subject transfers action to an inanimate object |
| | Nōntan. | *(You) hear it.* | |

The mode of a verb indicates the intention of the subject. For example, indicative mode denotes a statement of fact (*wāhsēyā* "it **is** sunny"), while the imperative mode gives a command (*kāhsīnincīn* "(you) **wash** your hands"). Other modes are introduced in the next section.

Verb Mode, Tense, and Aspect

MODE

The four verb types can be in the **indicative** mode, **subjunctive** mode, **negative indicative** mode, or **negative subjunctive** mode. Animate intransitive (AI), transitive animate (TA) and transitive inanimate (TI) are the only verbs that can be in the **imperative** and **negative imperative** modes.

The *indicative mode* can be used to make a statement or declaration or to ask polarity questions. Polarity questions are those that can be answered with a *yes* or *no*. The *negative indicative mode* is used to negate statements, and the *negative subjunctive mode* is used to negate subordinate clauses. The *imperative mode* is used for commands and suggestions, and the *negative imperative* is used to negate commands. The following are examples of the four verb types in the various modes:

Pēšik-išihsē.	*It is one o'clock.*	indicative
Kihci-sōkihpon.*	*It snows hard.*	indicative
Kihsinā mēkwā.*	*It is cold right now.*	indicative
Kimiwan na?	*Is it raining?*	polarity question
Kān kišāhtēhsinōn.	*It's not hot.*	negative indicative
Nipān!	*(You) sleep!*	imperative
Kēko nipāhkēn!	*(You) don't sleep!*	negative imperative
Mawi.	*She/he is crying.*	indicative
Kān mawihsī.	*She/he is not crying.*	negative indicative
Wīhsini na?	*Is she/he eating?*	polarity question
Kanawāpam anank.	*(You) look at the star!*	imperative
Kēko kanawāpamāhkēn anank!	*(You) don't look at the star!*	negative imperative
Niwāpamā nimāmā.	*I see my mother.*	indicative
Kān niwāpamāhsī nimāmā.	*I don't see my mother.*	negative indicative

* In these examples, *kihci-* "hard" is a pre-verb and *mēkwā* "right now" is a particle. They are used to add extra information about the situation, such as direction or manner. Pre-verbs and particles will be discussed in more detail in Chapter 9.

Kiwāpamā na?	*Do you see him/her/it?*	polarity question
Mīcin!	*(You) eat it!*	imperative
Kēko mīcihkēn!	*(You) don't eat it!*	negative imperative
Ninōntān.	*I hear it.*	indicative
Kān ninōntansīn.	*I don't hear it.*	negative indicative
Kiwāpantān na?	*Do you see it?*	polarity question

Subjunctive mode is used to express a hypothetical situation, a wish, a demand, or a suggestion. In Saulteaux, the subjunctive mode is used in subordinate clauses (a clause that cannot stand alone) and in supplementary questions.

Ahpī **kā-kimiwank...**	*When **it rained**...*
Ānīn **ēšiwēpahk** mēkwā?	*How **is the weather** right now?*
Awēnēn wīhsinit?	*Who (sg) is eating?*
Awēnēn amwāt?	*Who (sg) is eating it (NA)?*
Awēnēn mīcit?	*Who (sg) is eating it (NI)?*

TENSE AND ASPECT

Verbs also use different **tenses** and **aspects**. Tense indicates the time of an action, state, or event (past, present, or future). The examples above are in the *present tense* and indicate situations or events occurring at the time of speaking (now). The Saulteaux language displays the *present tense* (happening now), the *past tense* (has already happened), and the *future definite tense* (will definitely happen in the future).

Aspect considers qualities of an action or state independent of the tense. Saulteaux has *prospective aspect* (going to or intending to happen). Saulteaux indicates this with a pre-verb.

Conjugating Verbs

In an inflected language such as Saulteaux, **conjugation** is the variation of the form of a verb by which the mode, tense, number, and person are identified. For example, in English the verb "to swim" can be conjugated as *I swim, you swim, she swims, he swims, we swim,* or *they swim* (note the addition of *-s* on the 3rd person singular forms *she/he swims*.) To conjugate a verb is to make it agree with other words in a sentence. In Saulteaux, a personal prefix and/or a personal suffix is attached to the verb.

Each verb type has its own conjugation paradigm according to the mode, as in the above examples. The conjugation paradigms will be explained further in each of the verb chapters.

Inanimate intransitive verbs (V-II) in Saulteaux cannot be conjugated into the nine person forms because they use the inanimate subject *it*. This also means they cannot be put in the imperative or negative imperative forms because, for example, you cannot command the weather to be sunny.

Animate intransitive verbs (V-AI) are listed in the 3rd person singular (3s) *she/he*, and this is known as the "bare verb." These verbs end in the vowels (*i, ī, o, ō,* and *ā*) and in the consonants (*m* and *n*).

Nīm**i**.	*She/he is dancing.*
Anohk**ī**.	*She/he is working.*
Nakam**o**.	*She/he is singing.*
Pimipaht**ō**.	*She/he is running.*
Māc**ā**.	*She/he is leaving.*
Cīhkēnta**m**.	*She/he is happy.*
Nōntēhši**n**.	*She/he is tired.*

These are action and state verbs and can be conjugated in the nine person forms in all the modes and tenses. Only the personal suffixes will differ slightly depending on the verb ending.

Nīmi**n**!	*(You) dance!*	Imperative, 2s
<u>Kēko</u> anohkī<u>hkē</u>**n**!	*(You) <u>don't</u> work!*	negative imperative, 2s
Ninakam.	*I'm singing.*	indicative mode, 1s
<u>Kān</u> **ni**cīhkēnta<u>nsī</u>**min**.	*We are <u>not</u> happy.*	negative indicative, 1P
Kī-nōntēhšin**ōk**, kā-iškwā pimipahtō**wāt**.	*They were tired, after they ran.*	indicative, 1s / subjunctive, 1s
Ānīhšwīn wēnci-nōntēhšinsi**wan**?	*Why are **you** not tired?*	negative subjunctive, 2s

Transitive animate verbs (V-TA) are listed in the imperative singular (I.S.) *you*, and have various endings (*m, w, n, h, o, š,* and *hš*). These verbs can be conjugated in the nine person forms in all modes and with the tenses.

Wāpa**m**!	*(You) see him/her/it!*	
Nōnta**w**!	*(You) hear him/her/it!*	
Kipiti**n**!	*(You) stop him/her/it!*	
Wīci**h**!	*(You) help him/her/it!*	
Am**o**!	*(You) eat it* (NA)!	
Kanō**š**!	*(You) call him/her!*	
<u>Kēko</u> kanōnā<u>hkē</u>**n**!	*(You) <u>don't</u> call him/her/it!*	negative imperative, 2s
Ninōntawā.	*I hear him/her/it.*	indicative, 1s

Kān **owīcihāhsīn**.	*She/he is <u>not</u> helping him/her/it.*	negative indicative, 3s
Ānīhšwīn wēnci-kipitin**at**?	*Why did **you** stop him/her/it?*	subjunctive, 2s
Ānahpī amwāhsi**wānk** pahkwēšikan?	*When are **we** eating bannock?*	negative subjunctive, 1P

Transitive inanimate verbs (V-TI) are listed in the imperative singular (I.S.) *you* and have vowel stem endings (*a, i, ō*). These verbs can be conjugated in the nine person forms and they can be put in all the modes and the tenses.

Wāpanta**n**!	*(**You**) see it!*	
Mīci**n**!	*(**You**) eat it!*	
Pītō**n**!	*(**You**) bring it!*	
<u>Kēko</u> wāpanta<u>nkē</u>n!	*(**You**) <u>don't</u> see it!*	negative imperative, 2s
Nimīcin wīyāhs.	*I'm eating meat.*	indicative, 1s
Kān **ki**pītō<u>ns</u>īn.	*You are <u>not</u> bringing it.*	negative indicative, 2s
Ānahpī kā-wāpanta**nk** cīmān?	*When did **she/he** see a boat?*	subjunctive mode, 3s
Kīšpin mīci<u>hs</u>i**wānk**, kita-mīcin na?	*If **we** <u>don't</u> eat it, will you eat it?*	negative subjunctive, 1P

For extra practise, see the Chapter 8 Exercises on pages 161–162.

CHAPTER

· · · · · · · · · · ·

9

Objectives

- Particles
- Preverbs

Dialogues

1. Ānīn šikwa kīn?   *How are you now?*
   Kān kotinō, kīn tahs?   *Nothing wrong, you then?*
   Pēšikwan.   *The same.*

2. Ānahpī ēšāyan ōtēnānk?   *When are you going to town?*
   Mākišā wāpank.   *Maybe tomorrow.*

3. Kika-wāpamin mīnawā.   *I'll see you again.*
   Mīnankē, kika-wāpamin mīnawā.   *Yes, I'll see you again.*

Vocabulary

cīpwā	*before*	iškwāc	*last*
iškwā	*after*	pihcīnāko	*yesterday*
kēkā	*almost/just about*	pīnihš	*finally*
kēyāpi	*still/yet/ongoing*	šēmāk	*right away/immediately*

kikišēp	*this morning*	šikwa	*now*
cīkahī	*beside*	pimicahī	*alongside*
išpimink	*up/above*	pīncahī	*inside*
minšiwē	*all over*	pīntik	*inside/indoors*
nāwahī	*in the center/middle*	sīpāhahī	*under*
ānīhš	*why*	kotwā	*probably*
kayē	*also/too*	mākišā	*maybe*
kēhcinā	*probably*	onšām	*because*
kēmā	*or*	šikwa	*and*
kīšpin	*if*	tahs	*but/then*
ani-	*away from* (directional)	mācī-	*(to) start/beginning*
ci-	*can/able to*	mino-	*good/well/nice*

Introduction to Particles and Pre-verbs

Particles and pre-verbs are words or elements that have a grammatical function but do not fit into the main parts of speech (i.e., noun, verb, etc.). **Particles** typically encode grammatical categories (such as negation, mode, or tense) or act as fillers. They are never inflected, meaning they *do not change*. **Pre-verbs** attach directly to the verb and can change the meaning of the verb by adding new information.

PARTICLES

In Saulteaux, *particles* are words or elements that express notions of time, location, manner, degree, or circumstance, equivalent to the role that many *adverbs* and *prepositions* play in English. They are typically emphatic and expressive, and add detail or flavour to a phrase. Particles can occur before or after a verb, and some particles are only used with verbs in the subjunctive mode.

Kihsinā **nōnkom**.	*It is cold **today**.*	indicative
Āša kī-kīwē.	*She/he went home **already**.*	indicative
Wīnkē kišāhtē.	*It is **very** hot.*	indicative
Wēwīp, pimipahtōn!	***Hurry**, run!*	imperative
Kīšpin kīwēyan, nika-kaškēntam.	***If** you go home, I will be lonesome.*	subjunctive

Time/temporal particles specify the time or duration of an action, state, or event.

ahkawē	*first/beforehand*	nīkān	*first*
ahpī	*when/at that time*	nōmaya	*a little while ago*
āpitink	*once/one more time*	nōnkom	*today*
āša	*already*	pānimā	*later*

cīpwā	before		pēhkā	wait
iškwāc	last		pēhkiš	as well/all the while
iškwā	after		pihcīnāko	yesterday
kēkā	almost/just about		pīnihš	finally
kēyāpi	still/yet/ongoing		šēmāk	right away/immediately
kikišēp	this morning		šikwa	now
kīhtwām	again		tahšink	every time
kotink	at one time		tipihkahk	tonight
mēwinša	long ago		tipihkonk	last night
mīnawā	again		wāpank	tomorrow
mwētahš	after		wīhkā	ever
nēyāp	return/as before		wīpa	soon
nihšinē	always/all the time			

Locational particles specify the location of an action, event, or state.

akocīnk	outside/outdoors		okicahī	on top
anāmihī	underneath		pēhso	nearby
cīkahī	beside		pimicahī	alongside
išpimink	up/above		pīncahī	inside
minšiwē	all over		pīntik	inside/indoors
nāwahī	in the center/middle		sīpāhahī	under
nisahī	under/lower		wāhsa	far
nīkānahī	in front			

A few particles have similar forms as locative nouns, such as *akocīnk*. These are not classified as nouns. If the ending *-īnk* is removed, then *akoc-* has no meaning or word class.

Manner particles specify the way or manner in which an event, action, or state is carried out.

ēnikok	try hard		pahkān	different
ēniwēk	just so/so-so		pēšiko	alone
kēhtitawēn	suddenly		tāpiškō	just like
kīmōhc	on the sly/secretly		tānikanā	wishing
konakē	wondering		tēpināhk	any old way/carelessly/just enough
kwayak	correct/right		wēwēni	be careful/go slowly
māmāhšīhš	any old way/carelessly		wēwīp	hurry
māmow	together			

Degree particles specify the degree or intensity to which an event, action, or state is carried out.

āhpihci	very/really		kēkēt	really/surely
ēhta	only		wīnkē	really/very

Conjunctive particles serve to connect phrases, clauses, or sentences.

ānīhš	*why*	kotwā	*probably*
kayē	*also/too*	mākišā	*maybe*
kēhcinā	*probably*	onšām	*because*
kēmā	*or*	šikwa	*and*
kīšpin	*if*	tahs	*but/then*

Many of the particles above appear in more than one category, or they seem to overlap with particles in a different category. These can be used as either type of particle, depending on the context. A good example of this can be seen with the particle *šikwa*:

Pōsīns **šikwa** animohš.	*A cat **and** a dog.*	conjunctive particle
Kihsinā **šikwa.**	*It's cold **now**.*	temporal particle

The connector *tahs* can be translated as *but* or *then*, and it is used to link two parts of a sentence. In English, *but* is inserted between two parts of a sentence; in Saulteaux *tahs* comes after the first word in the second part of the sentence, as shown here:

Nimāmā anihšināpēmo, omaškīkōmo **tahs** kayē.	*My mother speaks Saulteaux, **but** she also speaks Swampy Cree.*
Niwīhsin, kīn **tahs**?	*I am eating, you **then**?*

The connective *kīšpin* "if" is used with the present indicative mood to refer to something that may be happening in the present:

Ani-kīwēn **kīšpin** ayēhkosiyan.	*Go home **if** you are tired.*

Kīšpin is also used with the unchanged present subjunctive mood to refer to future events:

Kika-išāmin **kīšpin** sōkihponsinok.	*We will go (there) **if** it doesn't snow.*

Some of these particles are used only with verbs in the subjunctive form.

Quantificational particles specify "how many" or general quantities and show similar grammatical behaviours as numbers.

ānint	*some*	nawac	*more/kind of*
kahkina	*all/everyone/everything*	nīpawa	*a lot/many*
kēkō	*something*	pankī	*a little*
nanāntok	*all kinds*		

Negative particles are particles that have a negative component in their meaning.

kāmahsi	*not yet*	kān kwayak	*not correct/not right*
kāwīn	*no*	kān pāhpiš	*not at all/not even*
kān awiya	*no one*	kān wīhkā	*never/not ever*

Interjectional particles serve to express emotions or evaluative attitudes.

ahām	*okay/all right*	mīkwēc	*thanks*
ampē	*come*	mīnankē	*yes*
awahš	*go away*	taka	*please*
awahšimē	*get worse*	wāhowa	*oh my*

When two elements are used together, such as the interrogative pronoun *ānīn* "how" and either particle *minik* or *tahso*, they are considered quantificational particles because they deal with quantities. The two particles are bound, meaning each needs another element with it to have a semantic meaning. *Ānīn minik* is used for asking "how much" and *ānīn tahso* is used for asking "how many."

Ānīn minik iwē papakowān?	*How much is that shirt?*
Ānīn tahso wāwanōn ēntawēntaman?	*How many eggs do you want?*

The predicate element or particle *mi-* "it is" or "so" is also used with verbs, pre-verbs, particles, demonstrative pronouns, and common names. This particle functions both as a focus-marker in constructions (also constructions with relative clauses) and as a discourse and sequencing device in narratives. Some examples are as follows:

Mi kī-tēpwēt.	***And so** he told the truth.*	verb
mi-iši	***and** then/**and** next*	pre-verb
mi-šikwa	***so** then*	particle
mi-awē	***it is** that (one)*	demonstrative pronoun
Mi John kā-tōtank naha?	***That's** what John did, right?*	common name

PRE-VERBS

Pre-verbs are words that add additional information to the verb such as directionality, or they can alter the semantics, therefore changing the meaning of the verb or phrase. Pre-verbs are always hyphenated, they occur in front of a verb, and they never occur alone.

ani-	*away from* (directional)	mācī-	*(to) start/beginning*
anta-	*go and…*	manki-	*big/huge* (only used with anatomy)
ci-	*can/able to*	mino-	*good/well/nice*
iši-	*to* (directional)	nōntē-	*to want*
kakwē-	*to try*	onci-	*from/for*
kihci-	*big/great/huge*	pi-	*toward/come* (directional)
maci-	*bad/evil*	pōni-	*to stop/quit*

The following are examples of inanimate intransitive verbs (V-II) and animate intransitive verbs (V-AI) with pre-verbs:

V-II

Kihci-kimiwan.	*It's raining **hard**.*
Mācī-sōkihpon.	*It's **starting** to snow.*

V-AI

Kakwē-antotan.	***Try** to listen.*
Ani-kīwēn.	***Go on** home.*
Kā-āpihtawohsēk nikī-**pi**-mācā.	*I left on Wednesday **to come here**.*
Kā-āpihtawohsēk nikī-mācā.	*I left on Wednesday (to go elsewhere).*
Apinōcīyak kī-**pi**-takohšinōk kā-mātinawē-kīšikahk.	*The children arrived **here** on Saturday.*
Pi-kīwēn cipwā-kimiwank.	***Come** home before it rains.*
Āša **ani**-awahšēwē kimihšōmihšinān.	*The sun is setting.* (lit., *Our grandfather is setting **out of sight**.*)

Compare the last five examples and notice how the presence and absence of *pi-* and *ani-* affect the meanings of the phrase. The pre-verb *pi-* indicates that something happens in the direction of the speaker, and ani- indicates something happens away from the speaker.

Cīpwā- "before" is sometimes used as a pre-verb when used with the unchanged present subjunctive mood, as in the second last example: *cipwā-kimiwank* "**before** it rains." Some of these words will also act as pre-nouns when used with nouns.

Tense markers are another type of pre-verb, which will be discussed in Chapter 10. For extra practise, see the Chapter 9 Exercises on page 163.

CHAPTER

· · · · · · · · · · ·

10

Objectives

- Inanimate intransitive verbs (V-II)
- Indicative mode—present tense
- Indicative mode—past tense and future definite tense
- Negative indicative mode

Dialogues

1. Ānīn šikwa kīn?
   Kān kotinō, kīn tahs?
   Pēšikwan.

   How are you now?
   Nothing wrong, you then?
   The same.

2. Kihsinā na mēkwā?
   Mīnankē, kihsinā, sōkihponānimat kayē.
   Pihcīnāko tahs, kī-kihsinā na?
   Kāwīn, wīnkē kī-āpawā.

   Is it cold right now?
   Yes, it's cold, and it's also blowing snow.
   Yesterday then, was it cold?
   No, it was very warm.

3. Kika-wāpamin mīnawā.
   Mīnankē, kika-wāpamin mīnawā.

   I'll see you again.
   Yes, I'll see you again.

4. Mātinawē-kīšikat na nōnkom?
   Kāwīn, nāno-kīšikat nōnkom.

   Is it Saturday today?
   No, it's Friday today.

5. Kikī-wīhsin na?
   Mīnankē, nikī-wīhsin nāwahkwēhk.

   Did you eat?
   Yes, I ate at noon.

Vocabulary

Kihsinā.	*It is cold.*
Wāhsēyā.	*It is sunny.*
Anamihē-kīšikat.	*It is Sunday.*
Nāno-kīšikat.	*It is Friday.*
Nāwihkwē.	*It is noon.*
Nīš-išihsē.	*It is two o'clock.*
Pipōn.	*It is winter.*
Nīpin.	*It is summer.*
Miskwā.	*It is red.*
Osāwā.	*It is yellow/brown.*

Inanimate Intransitive Verbs (V-II)

In this chapter, and in the next chapter, we will look at **inanimate intransitive** verbs, or V-II. This type of verb uses the *inanimate* subject "it," and so, unlike the other three verb types, it has no person or number and cannot be conjugated. An *intransitive* verb makes complete sense on its own and does *not* require a direct object, which means the verb does not transfer action to anything.

Kihsinā.	*It is cold.*

Indicative Mode—Present Tense

The **indicative mode** represents the denoted act or state. A verb in the indicative mode can be used to make a statement or declaration or to ask polarity questions, also known as *yes/no* questions because they can be answered with a yes or no. (These will be explained later in the chapter.) As with any mode, the verb will indicate the time or tense of the action, such as present, past, or future. We will look only at present tense for now.

Kihsinā mēkwā.	*It is cold right now.*
Sōkihpon nōnkom.	*It is snowing today.*

Examples of inanimate intransitive verbs (V-II) in Saulteaux include weather, days of the week, divisions of the day, time, seasons, and some colours.

WEATHER WORDS

Kimiwan.	*It is raining.*
Sōkihpon.	*It is snowing.*
Nōtin.	*It is windy.*
Awan.	*It is foggy.*
Kišāhtē.	*It is hot.* (outdoors)
Mino-kīšikat.	*It is a nice day.*
Kihsinā.	*It is cold.*
Wāhsēyā.	*It is sunny.*
Āpawā.	*It is warm.*
Awanipīhsā.	*It is drizzling.*
Kīšikāhtē.	*It is moonlight.*
Ninkwakwat.	*It is cloudy.*
Sōkihponānimat.	*It is blowing snow.*
Kotwāmihkwat.	*It is storming.*

DAYS OF THE WEEK

Most nouns and verbs in English are translated into Saulteaux as nouns and verbs, but note how the days of the week and divisions of the day are nouns in English but are inanimate intransitive verbs (V-II) in Saulteaux, just like the weather words, colours, and seasons.

Anamihē-kīšikat.	*It is Sunday.*	(lit., *It is prayer day.*)
Iškwā-anamihē-kīšikat.	*It is Monday.*	(lit., *It is a day after prayer day.*)
Nīšo-kīšikat.	*It is Tuesday.*	(lit., *It is the second day.*)
Āpihtawohsē.	*It is Wednesday.*	(lit., *It is mid-week.*)
Nīyo-kīšikat.	*It is Thursday.*	(lit., *It is the fourth day.*)
Nāno-kīšikat.	*It is Friday.*	(lit., *It is the fifth day.*)
Mātinawē-kīšikat.	*It is Saturday.*	(lit., *It is ration day.*)

For the days of the week, some dialects use *kīšikan* as well as *kīšikat*, but other dialects use the following:

Pēšiko-kīšikat.	*It is Monday.*	(lit., *It is the first day.*)
Nihso-kīšikat.	*It is Wednesday.*	(lit., *It is the third day.*)
Nikotwāhso-kīšikat.	*It is Saturday.*	(lit., *It is the sixth day.*)

DIVISIONS OF THE DAY

Saulteaux people of the past did not have clocks with which to tell time, so they divided the day into morning, noon, afternoon, evening, dusk, night, midnight, and dawn. The Saulteaux word for "clock," *kīhsohkān*, is derived from the word for "sun," *kīhsihs*, and the suffix *-hkan*, which indicates that something is artificial or fake. So the literal meaning is "artificial sun."

Mōhkahan.	*It is sunrise.*
Tipihkat.	*It is night.*
Kīšikat.	*It is day.*
Onāhkohšin.	*It is evening.*
Pankihšimon.	*It is sunset.*
Wāpan.	*It is dawn.*
Āpihtā-tipihkat.	*It is midnight.*
Nāwihkwē.	*It is noon.*

TIME

The Saulteaux word *išihsē* is used to express "hour," but it really means "it turns."

Pēšik-išihsē.	*It is one o'clock.*
Nīš-išihsē.	*It is two o'clock.*
Nihso-išihsē.	*It is three o'clock.*
Nīwin-išihsē.	*It is four o'clock.*
Nānan-išihsē.	*It is five o'clock.*
Nikotwāhso-išihsē.	*It is six o'clock.*
Nīšwāhso-išihsē.	*It is seven o'clock.*
Nihswāhso-išihsē.	*It is eight o'clock.*
Šānkahso-išihsē.	*It is nine o'clock.*
Mitāhso-išihsē.	*It is ten o'clock.*
Mitāhso ahsi pēšik-išihsē.	*It is eleven o'clock.*
Mitāhso ahsi nīš-išihsē.	*It is twelve o'clock.*

To put the time into half hours, the particles *mīnawā* "again" and *āpihta* "half" are inserted between the number and the verb. For example, in the sentence *Pēšik mīnawā āpihta-išihsēk ci-anta-anohkīyan nōnkom* "I have to go to work at 1:30 today," the Saulteaux phrase for 1:30 literally means "at one it turns and again at half."

The word for "minute" is *tipahikanēns* and plural "minutes" is *tipahikanēnsan*. This is an inanimate noun that refers to "little measurement(s)." It is never used for telling time but only for stating minutes.

pēšik tipahikanēns	*one minute*
Nika-pi-asēkīwē mitāhso tipahikanēnsan.	*I will return here in ten minutes.*
Mitāhso-išihsēk tipihkahk nika-kawišim.	*I will go to bed at ten tonight.*
Āša kēkā nānan-išihsē.	*It is almost five o'clock.*
Nīš-išihsēk iškwā-nāwihkwēk ci-mēkwāškawak nitōkimām.	*I have to meet with my boss at two this afternoon.*
Kika-māmawopimin ahpī wāpank kikišēp mitāhso išihsēk.	*We will have a meeting when/if it is 10:00 in the morning.*

SEASONS

Pipōn.	*It is winter.*
Sīkwan.	*It is spring.*
Nīpin.	*It is summer.*
Takwākin.	*It is autumn/fall.*

COLOURS

Colours are expressed as adjectives in English, but in Saulteaux they are expressed as verbs (some are V-II and others are V-AI). It must be kept in mind that the colour spectrum is a continuum, with each colour blending gradually into the one beside it, and each language divides this continuum differently, deciding which of the infinitely varied hues will be given the same name.

English imposes six basic divisions on the spectrum: red, orange, yellow, green, blue, and purple. Saulteaux requires a basic three-way division: *miskwā* "it's red," *osāwā* "it's yellow/ brown," and *osawaškwā* "it's blue/green." A non-Saulteaux speaker may find it strange to hear a Saulteaux speaker call orange *miskwū*. It must be remembered that Saulteaux is an old language, and many of the arbitrary distinctions between colours that are common now did not exist long ago.

The colours listed here are inanimate intransitive verbs in the indicative mode. The animate intransitive colours will be discussed later in the book.

Miskwā.	*It is red.*
Osāwā.	*It is yellow/brown.*
Osāwaškwā.	*It is blue/green.*
Wāpiškā.	*It is white.*
Mahkatēwā.	*It is black.*

Indicative Mode—Past Tense and Future Definite Tense

We've already seen examples in previous chapters of inanimate intransitive verbs (V-II) in indicative present tense. Now we will look at some examples in past tense and future definite tense.

PAST TENSE

The *past tense pre-verb* (kī-) indicates that something is completed, already done, or has already happened. The past tense pre-verb is always hyphenated when placed before a verb or another pre-verb in the indicative mode to make statements about events that occurred before the time of speaking. The following comments on the weather are in the indicative mode, past tense.

Kī-kimiwan.	*It rained.*
Wīnkē **kī**-kišāhtē.	*It was very hot.*
Wīnkē **kī**-kišāhtē nōnkom.	*It was very hot today.*
Kī-āpawā-tipihkat tipihkonk.	*Last night was a warm night.*

FUTURE DEFINITE TENSE

The *future definite tense pre-verb* (ta-) describes situations or events that are going to occur, or will occur, after the time of speaking. The following comments on the weather are in the indicative mode, future definite tense.

Ta-sōkihpon nōnkom.	*It will snow today.*
Mākišā **ta**-kišāhtē wāpank.	*Maybe it will be hot tomorrow.*
Ta-kišāhtē nōnkom.	*It will be hot today.*
Wīnkē **ta**-āpawā tipihkahk.	*It will be very warm tonight.*

Related to the future definite tense, the aspect pre-verb (wī-) indicates something is *going to* or is *intending to* be completed, with no reference to tense. The following comments on the weather are in the indicative mode, using the aspect pre-verb.

Wī-kimiwan.	*It is going to rain.*
Wīnkē **wī**-kišāhtē.	*It is going to be very hot.*
Mākišā **wī**-sōkihpon wāpank.	*Maybe it is going to snow tomorrow.*
Wī-kišāhtē nōnkom.	*It is going to be hot today.*

PRE-VERB ORDER

Tense pre-verbs come immediately *in front of* a verb. They can be removed from a verb and you would still have a complete verb form. In writing, a pre-verb is *always* separated from the verb by a hyphen. The hyphen indicates that the pre-verb is part of the word and adds grammatical meaning to the verb.

A tense pre-verb comes before another pre-verb as in the following statement:

Kī-	kihci-	sōkihpon.	*It snowed hard.*
(-ed)	*hard*	*It.snows*	
PAST TENSE			
PRE-VERB	PRE-VERB	VERB	

Two or more pre-verbs can be part of the same word, but you must know in which order to place them. There are also some verbs that have the same meaning as verbs with pre-verbs.

Māci-kimiwan.	*It is starting to rain.*	(one pre-verb)
Mācipihsā.	*It is starting to rain.*	
Kī-pōni-kimiwan.	*It stopped raining.*	(two pre-verbs)
Kī-pōnipīhsā.	*It stopped raining/drizzling.*	

PARTICLES

As we saw in the previous chapter, particles are used with verbs to provide certain additional information about a situation. Particles can occur *before* or *after* a verb.

Nōnkom kī-kimiwan.	*It rained **today**.*
Kī-kimiwan **nōnkom**.	*It rained **today**.*
Mākišā **nōnkom** ta-kihsinā.	*Maybe it will be cold **today**.*
Mākišā ta-kihsinā **nōnkom**.	*Maybe it will be cold **today**.*

POLARITY OR YES/NO QUESTIONS

Polarity questions are those to which the answer may be a simple *yes* or *no*. In Saulteaux, a yes/no question is formed from a statement by placing the word in question at the beginning of the sentence and placing the question indicator *na* after the word (also termed *na questions*).

Kimiwan.	*It is raining.*	(statement)
Kimiwan na?	*Is it raining?*	(yes/no question)

When asking a yes/no question, the question indicator *na* is always in the *second position* of a sentence or following the verb. The question indicator is used *only* in yes/no questions and *only* in the indicative mode. The following are polarity questions in the indicative mode regarding the weather.

Kimiwan **na**?	*Is it raining?*	Yes/No
Kimiwan **na** mēkwā?	*Is it raining right now?*	Yes/No
Wī-sōkihpon **na** mīnawā nōnkom?	*Is it going to snow again today?*	Yes/No
Kī-awanipīhsā **na** kikišēp?	*Was it drizzling this morning?*	Yes/No

Negative Indicative Mode

Another mode type that is used with weather words is the negative indicative mode. This mode is the opposite of the indicative mode. A situation is denied by using the particle *kāwīn* (or the collapsed form *kān*) "no/not" with an indicative verb, and at the same time adding a special suffix called a *negative suffix* to the verb. The negative suffix used with the weather words follows the pattern outlined below:

1. When the verb **ends in a vowel**, the negative suffix is *-hsinōn*

Kihsinā.	*It is cold.*
Kāwīn kihsinā**hsinōn**.	*It's **not** cold.*

2. When the verb **ends in a *t***, drop the *t* and add the negative suffix *-hsinōn*

Mino-kīšika**t**.	*It is a nice day.*
Kāwīn mino-kīšika**hsinōn**.	*It's **not** a nice day.*

3. When the verb **ends in an *n***, the negative suffix is *-sinōn*. When the suffix is added after *n*, the *n* becomes *nasalized*.

Kimiwa**n**.	*It is raining.*
Kāwīn kimiwa**nsinōn**.	*It's **not** raining.*

The following are examples of sentences in the negative indicative mode with various tenses and aspect regarding the weather.

Kāwīn kī-kihsinā**hsinōn**, kī-āpawā.	*It wasn't cold, it was warm.*
Kāwīn wī-mino-kīšika**hsinōn**.	*It is **not** going to be a nice day.*
Kāmahsi* pōni-kimiwa**nsinōn**.	*It didn't stop raining yet.*
Kāwīn ta-āpawā**hsinōn**.	*It will **not** be warm.*
Kāwīn sōkihpo**nsinōn** nōnkom.	*It is **not** snowing today.*

---

* Note that *kāmahsi* is the collapsed form of *kāwīn + mahsi*.

The following examples, statements, and yes/no questions are in the indicative and negative indicative mode with the various tenses and aspect.

Wīnkē kišāhtē nōnkom.	*It is very hot today.*
	(indicative present tense)
Nōnkom na āpawā?	*Is it warm today?*
	(indicative present tense)
Mīnankē wīnkē āpawā mēkwā.	*Yes, it's very warm today.*
	(indicative present tense)
Kī-sōkihpon tipihkonk.	*It snowed last night.*
	(indicative past tense)
Kāwīn, kī-kīšikāhtē.	*No, it was moonlight.*
	(negative indicative past tense)
Wī-kimiwan na wāpank?	*Is it going to rain tomorrow?*
	(indicative prospective aspect)
Kāwīn wī-kimiwansinōn wāpank.	*It's not going to rain tomorrow.*
	(negative indicative prospective aspect)
Kāwīn, kān ta-awansinōn.	*No, it will not be foggy.*
	(negative indicative future definite tense)

Three of the examples above contain the particle *kāwīn*, which in this context is used to state "no." In the last example where *kān* (*kāwīn* collapsed) is used, it is part of the negative indicative mode. For extra practise, see the Chapter 10 Exercises on page 164.

CHAPTER

• • • • • • • • • • •

11

Objectives

- Inanimate intransitive verbs (V-II), continued
- Subjunctive mode
- Negative subjunctive mode

Dialogues

1. Ānīn ēšiwēpahk mēkwā?   *How is the weather right now?*
   Wāhsēyā.   *It is sunny.*

2. Kimiwan na?   *Is it raining?*
   Mīnankē kimiwan.   *Yes, it's raining.*

3. Ānīn wā-išiwēpahk wāpank?   *How is the weather going to be tomorrow?*
   Wī-nōtin wāpank.   *It's going to be windy tomorrow.*

4. Sōkihpon na?   *Is it snowing?*
   Kāwīn sōkihponsinōn.   *It's not snowing.*

Vocabulary

kišāhtēhk	*it is hot...*	awanipīhsāhk	*it drizzles...*
ninkwakwahk	*it is cloudy...*	awank	*it is foggy...*
wāwāhsikonēhsēhk	*it is lightning...*	anankōnskāhk	*it's starry...*
Mino-kīšikat.	*It is a nice day.*	mino-kīšikahsinohk	*it is not a nice day...*
Kihsinā.	*It is cold.*	kihsināhsinohk	*it is not cold...*

Inanimate Intransitive Verbs (V-II), continued

Chapter 10 introduced inanimate intransitive verbs (V-II) in the indicative and negative indicative modes. In this chapter, we will look at inanimate intransitive verbs in the subjunctive and negative subjunctive modes, exploring weather words and supplementary questions.

Subjunctive Mode

Subjunctive mode is a verb mode used to indicate subordination and is considered less "factual" than the indicative mode. The subjunctive mode is used in subordinate clauses and in supplementary questions.

A **subordinate clause** cannot stand alone because it relies on the main part of the sentence to be grammatical. In the following English example, the main clause, *Tim likes to walk*, is a complete thought and can stand alone. The subordinate clause, *when it rains*, is not a complete thought and is dependent on the main clause.

Tim likes to walk	when it rains.
MAIN CLAUSE	SUBORDINATE CLAUSE

Supplementary questions begin with interrogative pronouns (for a review of these, see chapter 5) and must be supplemented with an answer. In this mode, the verbs take a subjunctive suffix. In the following supplementary question about the weather, the verb is in the subjunctive mode.

Ānīn ēšiwēpahk mēkwā?	*How is the weather right now?*

The subjunctive suffixes for all V-IIs are either -*(n)k* or -*hk*. For verbs that end in –*n*, the subjunctive suffix is -*(n)k*:

Kimiwa**n**.	*It is raining.*	indicative
kimiwa**nk**	*it rains...*	subjunctive

There are two exceptions to this rule. For the verbs sōkihpon and wāpan, the subjunctive suffix is *-hk*:

Sōkihpo**n**.	*It is snowing.*	indicative
sōkihpo**hk**	*it snows...*	subjunctive
Wāpa**n**.	*It is dawn.*	indicative
wāpa**hk**	*it is dawn...*	subjunctive

For V-IIs that end in a vowel, the suffix is also *-hk*:

Wāhsēyā.	*It is sunny.*	indicative
wāhsēyā**hk**	*it is sunny...*	subjunctive

For V-IIs that end in –*t*, the *-t* must be dropped before adding the suffix *-hk*:

Mino-kīšika**t**.	*It is a nice day.*	indicative
mino-kīšika**hk**	*it is a nice day...*	subjunctive

WEATHER WORDS—SUBJUNCTIVE MODE

mino-kīšika**hk**	*it is a nice day...*	kišāhtē**hk**	*it is hot...*
ninkwakwa**hk**	*it is cloudy...*	kihsinā**hk**	*it is cold...*
sōkihponānima**hk**	*it blows snow...*	āpawā**hk**	*it is warm...*
nōti**nk**	*it is windy...*	awanipīhsā**hk**	*it drizzles...*
kimiwa**nk**	*it rains...*	wāhsēyā**hk**	*it is sunny...*
awa**nk**	*it is foggy...*	kīšikāhtē**hk**	*it is moonlight...*
sōkihpo**hk**	*it snows...*	wāwāhsikonēhsē**hk**	*it is lightning...*
anankōnskā**hk**	*it's starry...*	nānāhtē**hk**	*Northern lights*

For some words, the translation is the same in both indicative and subjunctive modes, but the difference between the modes is the context in which they are used. The following sentences show the difference between a statement in the indicative and a yes/no question in the indicative:

Wī-mino-kīšikat wāpank.	*It's going to be a nice day tomorrow.*
Wī-kihsinā na mīnawā wāpank?	*Is it going to be cold again tomorrow?*

The following sentences contain subordinate clauses in which the verbs are in the subjunctive mode. The first sentence contains a *conditional clause* (starting with *if*) and the second sentence contains a *result clause* (starting with *when*). If these clauses are left alone, they are ungrammatical.

Kīšpin **mino-kīšikahk** wāpank, nika-išā ōtēnānk.	*If **it's a nice day** tomorrow, I will go to town.*
Nikī-nipā pihcīnāko ahpī **kā-kimiwank**.	*I slept yesterday when **it rained**.*

In each of the following examples, the verb in sentence 1) is in the indicative mode, and the verb in sentence 2) is in the subjunctive mode.

1. Kī-kihci-nōtin mīnawā tipihkonk.   *It was very windy again last night.*
2. Kahkina nikī-apimin kā-kihci-nōtink.   *We were all home when it was very windy.*

1. Wī-kišāhtē wāpank.   *It is going to be hot tomorrow.*
2. Kāwīn nika-anohkīhsī kīšpin kišāhtēhk.   *I will not work if it's hot.*

1. Kī-sōkihponānimat kikišēp.   *It was blowing snow this morning.*
2. Nikī-ayap ahpī kā-sōkihponānimahk.   *I was at home when it was blowing snow.*

SUPPLEMENTARY QUESTIONS

Supplementary questions in Saulteaux begin with interrogative pronouns, as we saw in chapter 5. You will remember that most of those pronouns begin with *ān*, so they can be referred to as *ān*-questions. In Saulteaux a verb has to be in the subjunctive mode when asking supplementary questions.

Ānahpī kā-āpawāhk?	*When was it warm?*
Ānahpī mīnawā kē-kihsināhk?	*When will it be cold again?*

The tense and aspect pre-verbs change when used in supplementary questions. The pre-verbs go through an initial change in which the vowel changes from *ī* → *ā* when a tense pre-verb is used in the subjunctive mood. The tense and aspect pre-verbs for the subjunctive mode are as follows:

Indicative → Subjunctive mode (V-II)

present	no pre-verb
past	kī → kā-
future definite (will)	ka → àkē-
aspect (going to)	wī → wā-

Although there is a tendency to answer supplementary questions with *mīnankē* or *kāwīn*, for practice it is better to answer in full statements.

Q:	Kimiwan na?	*Is it raining?*	
A:	Mīnankē kimiwan.	*Yes, it's raining.*	affirmative
	Kāwīn kimiwansinōn.	*It's not raining.*	negative

Q:	Sōkihpon na?	*Is it snowing?*	
A:	Mīnankē sōkihpon.	*Yes, it's snowing.*	affirmative
	Kāwīn sōkihponsinōn.	*It's not snowing.*	negative

The following are supplementary questions about the weather and some responses to the questions. You can substitute the weather word according to the weather on any specific day.

1. Ānīn ēšiwēpahk mēkwā?   *How is the weather right now?*
   Āpawā mēkwā.   *It's warm right now.*

2. Ānīn kā-išiwēpahk pihcīnāko? *How was the weather yesterday?*
   Kī-kihsinā pihcīnāko.   *It was cold yesterday.*

3. Ānīn wā-išiwēpahk wāpank?   *How is the weather going to be tomorrow?*
   Wī-nōtin wāpank.   *It's going to be windy tomorrow.*

4. Ānīn kē-išiwēpahk wāpank?   *How will the weather be tomorrow?*
   Kāwīn wī-kimiwansinōn wāpank, *It's not going to rain tomorrow, it will be a nice day.*
   ta-mino-kīšikat.

Negative Subjunctive Mode

Negative subjunctive mode is the opposite of the subjunctive mode, in that it is used to negate subordinate clauses and supplementary questions. This mode *does not need* the particle *kāwīn* "no/not" before the verb. It attaches a suffix to the verb called a **negative suffix**. The negative suffixes used with the weather words are as follows:

1. When the verb ends in a vowel, add the suffix *-hsino*(-*hk*)

Kihsinā.			*It is cold.*
kihsinā	+ -hsino	+ -hk	
VERB	+ NEG. SF	+ SUBJ. SF	
kihsināhsinohk			*it is not cold...*

Kišpin **kihsināhsinohk**, ōtēnank   *If **it's not cold**, I am going to go to town tomorrow.*
   niwī-išā wāpank.

2. When the verb ends in -n, add the suffix *-sinon(-hk)*

Kimiwan.		*It is raining.*
kimiwan	+ -sinon	+ -hk
VERB	+ NEG. SF	+ SUBJ. SF
kimiwansinohk		*it is not raining...*

Wīnkē kī-kihci-ninkwakwat, ānihšwīn   *It was very cloudy, (I) wonder why **it didn't rain**.*
  ītok wēnci-kī-**kimiwansinohk**.

3. When the verb ends in a -t, drop the -t and add the suffix *-hsino(-hk)*

Mino-kīšikat.		*It is a nice day.*
mino-kīšika	+ -hsino	+ -hk
VERB	+ NEG. SF	+ (SUBJ. SF)
mino-kīšikahsinohk		*it is not a nice day...*

Kīšpin wi-**mino-kīšikahsinohk**   *If **it's not** going to be **nice** tomorrow,*
  wāpank, kāwīn niwī-anohkīhsī.   *I'm not going to work.*

Inanimate intransitive verbs (V-II) cannot be conjugated, which means they cannot be put in the nine person forms like the other verb types, AI, TI, and TA. This chart shows that the various forms for each mode for II verbs are always in 3rd person singular.

Subject	Indicative	Subjunctive	Negative indicative	Negative subjunctive	Obviative
1s -----	-------	-------	-------	-------	-------
2s -----	-------	-------	-------	-------	-------
3s it	kihsinā *it's cold*	kihsināhk *(if) it's cold*	kihsināhsinōn *it's not cold*	kihsināhsinohk *(if) it's not cold*	kihsinānik *it's cold*
3's ----	-------	-------	-------	-------	-------
1P -----	-------	-------	-------	-------	-------
21 ----	-------	-------	-------	-------	-------
2P -----	-------	-------	-------	-------	-------
3P -----	-------	-------	-------	-------	-------
3'P ----	-------	-------	-------	-------	-------

For extra practise, see the Chapter 11 Exercises on page 165.

CHAPTER

12

Objectives

- Animate intransitive verbs (V-AI)
- Imperative and negative imperative modes
- Indicative mode
- Negative indicative mode

Dialogues

1. Ānīn ēntōtaman?   *What are you doing?*
   Nitanamihcikē mēkwā.   *I'm reading right now.*
   Kēko anamihcīkēhkēn, pi-otaminon.   *Don't read, come play.*

2. Wēkonēn wāpantaman?   *What do you see?*
   Kān niwāpantansīn kēkō.   *I don't see anything.*

3. Kēko niškātēntankēk, pāhpik!   *Don't be sad, laugh!*
   Mīnankē, cīhkēntantā šikwa nīmitā!   *Yes, let's be happy and (let's) dance!*

Vocabulary

Antotan.	*Listen.*	Pankitōn.	*Be quiet.*
Apin.	*Sit.*	Pimipahtōn.	*Run.*

Mawin.	*Cry.*	Pimohsēn.	*Walk.*
Kīwēk.	*(you all) Go home.*	Sākahantā.	*Let's go outside.*
Pīntikēk.	*(you all) Come in.*	Minihkwētā.	*Let's drink.*
Nakamok.	*(you all) Sing.*	Wīhsinitā.	*Let's eat.*
Kēko kīwēhkēn.	*Don't go home.*	Kēko išātā.	*Let's not go (there).*
Kēko antotankēn.	*Don't listen.*	Anohkī.	*She/he is working.*
Nitanohkī.	*I'm working.*	Kitōtamin.	*You are playing.*

Animate Intransitive Verbs (V-AI)

As mentioned before, a verb is a part of speech that describes an action, state, or event. In chapters 10 and 11 we looked at inanimate intransitive verbs and their various modes. **Animate intransitive verbs** (V-AI) are another type of intransitive verb in the Saulteaux language. These verbs have an *animate* subject and *no* direct object, so no action is transferred to anyone or anything.

> pīntikē   *she/he is entering/coming in/going in*

In the example above, the animate subject of the verb *enter* is *she/he*, and there is no *direct object* and no action being transferred to anyone or anything. The verb is in the indicative mode, 3rd person singular, also referred to as the "bare verb."

Saulteaux animate intransitive verbs are actions, states of being, and some colours. As with the V-II type, these verbs also have different modes. This chapter will introduce the imperative, negative imperative, indicative, and negative indicative modes for V-AIs. Chapter 13 will focus on the subjunctive and negative subjunctive modes for V-AIs.

Imperative and Negative Imperative Modes

The **imperative mode** is used to issue a *command* or a *suggestion* at the time of speaking or in the present. The **negative imperative mode** is used to negate a command. In the Saulteaux language, there are six imperative forms: three imperative singular and three imperative plural. These forms also distinguish between singular and plural "you." The following table lists the abbreviations used to indicate the patterns.

I.S.	Imperative Singular	said to one person
I.P.	Imperative Plural	said to more than one person
I.I.	Imperative Inclusive	said to us, me including you
N.I.S.	Negative Imperative Singular	said to one person
N.I.P.	Negative Imperative Plural	said to more than one person
N.I.I.	Negative Imperative Inclusive	said to us, me including you

The imperative suffixes are attached to the verb. For the negative imperative forms, the particle *kēko* "don't" is always used and is placed before the verb. The following tables will illustrate three animate intransitive verb patterns in the six forms.

V–AI ending in any vowel (*a, ā, i, ī, o, ō, ē*)		
I.S.	_____-n	*you (sg)...*
I.P.	_____-k	*you all (pl)...*
I.I.	_____-tā	*let's...*
N.I.S.	kēko _____-hkēn	*(you) don't (sg)...*
N.I.P.	kēko _____-hkēk	*(you all) don't (pl)...*
N.I.I.	kēko _____-tā	*let's not...*

nipā – *she/he is sleeping*

nipān	*(you) sleep*
nipāk	*(you all) sleep*
nipātā	*let's sleep*
kēko nipāhkēn	*(you) don't sleep*
kēko nipāhkēk	*(you all) don't sleep*
kēko nipātā	*let's not sleep*

V–AI ending in *–am*		
I.S.	_____-n	*you (sg)...*
I.P.	_____-ok	*you all (pl)...*
I.I.	_____-ntā	*let's...*
N.I.S.	kēko _____-nkēn	*(you) don't (sg)...*
N.I.P.	kēko _____-nkēk	*(you all) don't (pl)...*
N.I.I.	kēko _____-ntā	*let's not...*

tōtam – *she/he does so*

tōta**n**	*(you) do so*
tōta**mok***	*(you all) do so*
tōta**ntā**	*let's do so*
kēko tōta**nkēn**	*(you) don't do so*
kēko tōta**nkēk**	*(you all) don't do so*
kēko tōta**ntā**	*let's not do so*

V-AI ending in –hšin		
I.S.	_____ -in	*you (sg)…*
I.P.	_____ -ik	*you all (pl)…*
I.I.	_____ -itā	*let's…*
N.I.S.	kēko _____ -ihkēn	*(you) don't (sg)…*
N.I.P.	kēko _____ -ihkēk	*(you all) don't (pl)…*
N.I.I.	kēko _____ -itā	*let's not…*

takohšin – *she/he is arriving*

takohšin**in**	*(you) arrive*
takohšin**ik**	*(you all) arrive*
takohšin**itā**	*let's arrive*
kēko takohšin**ihkēn**	*(you) don't arrive*
kēko takohšin**ihkēk**	*(you all) don't arrive*
kēko takohšin**itā**	*let's not arrive*

Here are some examples of V-AIs in the imperative singular (I.S.):

Antotan.	*Listen.*	Pankitōn.	*Be quiet.*
Apin.	*Sit.*	Pimipahtōn.	*Run.*
Mawin.	*Cry.*	Pimohsēn.	*Walk.*
Minihkwēn.	*Drink.*	Pīntikēn.[†]	*Enter/come in/go in.*
Nakamon.	*Sing.*	Sākahan.[‡]	*Go outside.*
Nīmin.	*Dance.*	Wēpahikēn.	*Sweep.*
Nīpawin.	*Stand.*	Wīhsinin.	*Eat.*
Omā-pi-išān.[§]	*Come here.*		

* For this type of verb, the final -*m* is dropped and the suffix is attached, except in the imperative plural form, where the -*m* is kept.

† This word is used where English uses "come in" to invite someone at the door to come into or enter the building or room. Another, more exact, translation for "come in" is *pi-pīntikēn* (singular) and *pi-pīntikēk* (plural).

‡ To some speakers this word means "go to the bathroom/outhouse." Such speakers would use *akocīnk išān* for "go outside" and *akocīnk išāk* for "(you all) go outside"; literally, this means "outdoors, go there."

§ Another word for "come here," besides *omā-pi-išān*, is *ampē* "come" or *ampē omā* "come here." *Ampē* is not a verb but an interjection, and therefore it cannot be conjugated.

Here are some examples of V-AIs in the imperative plural (I.P.):

Antotamok.	*(you all) Listen.*	Omā-pī-išāk.	*(you all) Come here.*
Apik.	*(you all) Sit.*	Pankitōk.	*(you all) Be quiet.*
Kīwēk.	*(you all) Go home.*	Pimipahtōk.	*(you all) Run.*
Nakamok.	*(you all) Sing.*	Pīntikēk.	*(you all) Enter/come in.*
Nīmik.	*(you all) Dance.*	Sākahamok.	*(you all) Go outside.*

Here are some examples of V-AIs in the imperative inclusive (I.I.):

Apitā.	*Let's sit.*	Nīmitā.	*Let's dance.*
Cīhkēntantā.	*Let's be happy.*	Pimipahtōtā.	*Let's run.*
Kīwētā.	*Let's go home.*	Pīntikētā.	*Let's enter/come in.*
Minihkwētā.	*Let's drink.*	Sākahantā.	*Let's go outside.*
Nakamotā.	*Let's sing.*	Wīhsinitā.	*Let's eat.*

Note that some dialects will use *-tāk* instead of *-tā* for the inclusive form, as in the example *pīntikētāk* "let's enter/go in."

Here are some examples of negative imperative in singular, plural, and inclusive. Can you tell which is which?

Kēko pīntikēhkēk.	*(you all) Don't enter.*	Kēko išāhkēn.	*Don't go (there).*
Kēko imā pīntikētā.	*Let's not enter there.*	Kēko apitā.	*Let's not sit.*
Kēko apihkēn.	*Don't sit/stay home.*	Kēko mācāhkēn.	*Don't leave.*
Kēko kīwēhkēn.	*Don't go home.*	Kēko išātā.	*Let's not go (there).*
Kēko antotankēn.	*Don't listen.*	Kēko antotantā.	*Let's not listen.*

DELAYED IMPERATIVE

The **delayed imperative** is a mode that is used to give commands that will take place at a "later" time. The following chart lists the delayed imperative suffixes for the singular, plural, and inclusive forms. Note that either the particle *pānimā* "later" or the pre-verb *cīpwā* "before" is usually used with the verb in this mood.

Delayed Imperative forms		
I.S.	pānimā (verb)-hkan	*(you)...later*
I.P.	pānimā (verb)-hkēk	*(you all)...later*
I.I.	pānimā (verb)-hkank	*let's ...later*

Pānimā kīwēhka**n**.	*(you) Go home later.*
Pānimā kīwēh**kēk**.	*(you all) Go home later.*
Pānimā kīwēh**kank**.	*Let's go home later.*
Wīhsini**hkan** cīpwā-mācāyan.	*Eat before you leave.*
Pānimā kīnawā wīhsini**hkēk**.	*Eat later, you all.*

Imperatives, negative imperatives, and delayed imperatives can be used with pre-verbs and particles. For a review, see Chapter 9.

Indicative Mode

As mentioned before, the indicative mode is used to make statements and ask polarity (yes/no) questions. Animate intransitive verbs in the indicative do not transfer an action onto a direct object, and they can be conjugated into the nine forms based on the subject paradigms below. V-AIs are always listed in the 3rd person form, or the "bare verb" form.

Personal pronouns are used with a verb to express the subject of the sentence and the one who does the action. As we saw in Chapter 5, personal pronouns in Saulteaux are all affixes. Affixes in the indicative mode are called *indicative personal affixes*, and the following table outlines the form of the indicative personal affix used with V-AIs. The personal prefixes and suffixes are shown with hyphens in the paradigm to indicate that they are attached to the beginning or at the end of the verb.

No.	Subject	Indicative personal affix
1s	*I*	ni-(verb)
2s	*you*	ki-(verb)
3s	*she/he*	(bare verb)
3's	*his/her ___*	(verb)-wan
1P	*we* (ex)	ni-(verb)-min
21	*we* (in)	ki-(verb)-min
2P	*you all*	ki-(verb)-m
3P	*they*	(verb)-wak
3'P	*his/her ___s*	(verb)-wah

This is the basic paradigm for V-AI, but remember that in the indicative form there are rules that apply for verbs that begin with a vowel and for verbs that end with short vowels or with certain consonants. Another way of understanding the paradigm of verbs is to see the nature of the utterance, as in who speaks, who is spoken *to*, and who is spoken *about*.

1st person subject: the speaker	2nd person subject: the one/ones spoken to	3rd person subject: the one/ones talked about
1s ni- the speaker talks about him/herself: *I*	**2s ki-** the addressee, i.e., the one spoken to: *you*	**3s bare verb** the topic, i.e., the one spoken about: *she/he*
1P ni- -min the speaker talks about self and others, but excludes the one spoken to: *we* (ex)	**2P ki- -m** two or more persons are spoken to: *you all*	**3P -wak** two or more persons are spoken about: *they*
21 ki- -min the speaker talks about self and others and includes the one spoken to: *we* (in)		**3's -wan** the friend, relative or pet of a 3rd person: *his/her* ____
		3'P -wah the friends, relatives or pets of a 3rd person: *his/her* ____s

(Table adapted from Solomon Ratt)

The following are examples of verbs in the indicative mode.

Anohkīwak nōnkom.	*They are working today.*
Kitayap na nōnkom?	*Are you at home today?*
Nōnkom na kicīhkēntam?	*Are you happy today?*
Animohš šinkihšin.	*The dog is lying down.*

The rules for conjugating the various animate intransitive verb stems in the indicative mode are as follows:

1. When conjugating verbs that **begin with a vowel in the bare verb** form (3rd sg), the 1st and 2nd person forms are *nit-* and *kit-* instead of *ni-* and *ki-*. The *-t-* serves as a connector between two vowels. This only occurs in the *indicative* and *negative indicative* modes in *present tense*. If the verb begins with the short vowel "o," the vowel becomes long (ō).

anohkī	*she/he is working*	(3rd per sg)
nitanohkī	*I'm working*	(1st per sg)
*o*tamino	*she/he is playing*	(3rd per sg)
kit*ō*tamin	*you are playing*	(2nd per sg)

2. When conjugating verbs that *end in the short vowels i and o*, drop the final vowel in the 1st and 2nd persons singular only. This only occurs in the *indicative mode*.

wīhsin*i*	*she/he is eating*	(3rd per sg)
niwīhsin_	*I'm eating*	(1st per sg)

Remember: when conjugating verbs that *begin with a vowel* and *end in the short vowels*, both rules apply.

ap*i*	*she/he is sitting*	(3rd per sg)
kitap_	*you are sitting*	(2nd per sg)

3. When conjugating verbs that *end in -am and -hšin*, the 3rd person obviative singular (3'S) and the 3rd person obviative plural (3'P) *will not* take the person suffixes -*wan* and –*wah*; they will take the person suffixes -*ōn* and -*ōh*. The 3rd person plural (3P) *will not* take the person suffix -*wak*; it will take the person suffix -*ōk*.

3s	wīhsini	*she/he is eating*
3's	wīhsini**wan**	*his/her _____ is eating*
3P	wīhsini**wak**	*they are eating*
3'P	wīhsini**wah**	*his/her _____s are eating*

3s	cīhkēnt*am*	*she/he is happy*
3's	cīhkēntam**ōn**	*his/her _____ is happy*
3P	cīhkēntam**ōk**	*they are happy*
3'P	cīhkēntam**ōh**	*his/her _____s are happy*

3s	takoh*šin*	*she/he is arriving*
3's	takohšin**ōn**	*his/her _____ is arriving*
3P	takohšin**ōk**	*they are arriving*
3'P	takohšin**ōh**	*his/her _____s are arriving*

The following tables contain the various V-AI stems in the indicative mode paradigms. The verbs are all in the present tense (tense will be discussed in the next section).

V-AI Indicative Present Tense

api – *she/he is sitting*

1s	**nit**ap	*I am sitting*
2s	**kit**ap	*you are sitting*
3s	api	*she/he is sitting*
3's	api**wan**	*his/her _____ is sitting*
1P	**nit**api**min**	*we* (ex) *are sitting*
21	**kit**api**min**	*we* (in) *are sitting*
2P	**kit**api**m**	*you all are sitting*
3P	api**wak**	*they are sitting*
3'P	api**wah**	*his/her ____s are sitting*

The bare verb *api* begins in a vowel; therefore, the connector *-t-* is inserted in the 1st and 2nd persons only (singular and plural). The verb also ends in a short vowel; therefore, the short final vowel is deleted in the 1st and 2nd person singular *only*. For verbs that end in long vowels, the long final vowel is not deleted.

otamino – *she/he is playing*

1s	**nit**ōtamin	*I am playing*
2s	**kit**ōtamin	*you are playing*
3s	otamino	*she/he is playing*
3's	otamino**wan**	*his/her _____ is playing*
1P	**nit**ōtamino**min**	*we* (ex) *are playing*
21	**kit**ōtamino**min**	*we* (in) *are playing*
2P	**kit**ōtamino**m**	*you all are playing*
3P	otamino**wak**	*they are playing*
3'P	otamino**wah**	*his/her ____s are playing*

The bare verb *otamino* begins in a short vowel *o-*; therefore, the vowel becomes long when the personal prefix with the connector *-t-* is attached, in the 1st and 2nd persons only. The verb also ends in a short vowel; therefore, the short final vowel is deleted in the 1st and 2nd person singular *only*.

takohšin – *she/he is arriving*

1S	**ni**takohšin	*I am arriving*
2S	**ki**takohšin	*you are arriving*
3S	takohšin	*she/he is arriving*
3'S	takohšin**ōn**	*his/her _____ is arriving*
1P	**ni**takohšin**imin**	*we (ex) are arriving*
21	**ki**takohšin**imin**	*we (in) are arriving*
2P	**ki**takohšin**im**	*you all are arriving*
3P	takohšin**ōk**	*they are arriving*
3'P	takohšin**ōh**	*his/her ____s are arriving*

The connective "t" is not needed with verbs that begin in consonants, such as *takohšin*. An "i" is inserted after the verb and before the personal suffixes in the 1st and 2nd persons plural for verbs that end in -*hšin*. The 3rd persons (singular and plural) personal suffixes differ from verbs that end in vowels.

sākaham – *she/he is going outside*

1S	**ni**sākaham	*I am going outside*
2S	**ki**sākaham	*you are going outside*
3S	sākaham	*she/he is going outside*
3'S	sākaham**ōn**	*his/her _____ is going outside*
1P	**ni**sākahā**min**	*we (ex) are going outside*
21	**ki**sākahā**min**	*we (in) are going outside*
2P	**ki**sākahā**m**	*you all are going outside*
3P	sākaham**ōk**	*they are going outside*
3'P	sākaham**ōh**	*his/her ____s are going outside*

For verbs ending in –*am*, such as *sākaham*, the short "a" becomes long "ā" in the 1st person plural (1P) and 2nd persons inclusive and plural (21 and 2P). Again, the 3rd person personal suffixes differ with this verb ending.

TENSE AND ASPECT

As mentioned before, tense indicates the time of an action, state, or event, and aspect considers the qualities of an action or state independent of the tense. The tenses are *present tense* (happening now), *past tense* (has already happened), *future definite tense* (will definitely happen in the future), and *aspect* (is going to happen without reference to time).

All tense/aspect indicators can be placed after the personal prefix and before the pre-verbs, verb root, and verb suffix, as shown in the following paradigm. The standard verb structure for V-AI follows this pattern:

Personal prefix	Tense/aspect pre-verbs	Pre-verbs	Verb root/stem	Verb suffix
ni(t)-	kī-			
ki(t)-	ka-			
	ta-			
	wī-			

In the Saulteaux language, the verb is the most important element, as it takes on the tense/aspect, person, number (singular/plural), mode, and modifiers (pre-verbs). Anything else before or after the verb is a noun, pronoun, pre-noun or particle.

With the V-II, we had only one form for the future definite tense, but with the other verbs types—AI, TI and TA—there are *two* future definite tense indicators. The future definite tense for 1st and 2nd person forms is *ka-*, and the future definite tense for 3rd person forms is *ta-*. These tenses are never used with the subjunctive forms of verbs. The tenses for the subjunctive forms differ.

Tense/Aspect Pre-verbs – Indicative Mode		
Tense	**Pre-verb**	**Example**
Present	none	niwaniškā – *I am rising from bed*
Past	kī-	nikī-waniškā – *I rose from bed*
Future definite (will)	ka- (1st and 2nd pers) ta- (3rd pers)	nika-waniškā – *I will rise from bed* ta-waniškā – *she/he will rise from bed*
Aspect	**Pre-verb**	**Example**
Future intentive (going to)	wī-	niwī-waniškā – *I'm going to rise from bed*

When adding tense/aspect to verbs in the indicative mode, the tense/aspect pre-verb comes after the personal prefix and before (pre-) the verb and is always hyphenated. Pre-verbs are always hyphenated to indicate that it is part of the verb and can be removed from the verb. For some verbs in English, the past tense is a suffix, and for others, a change occurs in the word:

bare verb:	work	run
past:	work**ed**	ran

In Saulteaux, person and tense/aspect are attached to the verb:

person	**+ tense**	**+ verb**	**+ suffix**		
ni-	+ kī-	+ anohkī		= nikī-anohkī	*I worked*
ni-	+ kī-	+ anohkī	+ min	= nikī-anohkīmin	*we worked*

The following tables show examples of AI verbs in the person paradigms in the indicative mode: past tense, future definite tense, and aspect.

V-AI Indicative Past Tense

pāhpi – *she/he is laughing*

1S	nikī-pāhp	*I laughed*
2S	kikī-pāhp	*you laughed*
3S	kī-pāhpi	*she/he laughed*
3's	kī-pāhpiwan	*his/her _____ laughed*
1P	nikī-pāhpimin	*we (ex) laughed*
21	kikī-pāhpimin	*we (in) laughed*
2P	kikī-pāhpim	*you all laughed*
3P	kī-pāhpiwak	*they laughed*
3'P	kī-pāhpiwah	*his/her _____s laughed*

V-AI Indicative Future Definite Tense (will)

wīhsini – *she/he is eating*

1S	nika-wīhsin	*I will eat*
2S	kika-wīhsin	*you will eat*
3S	ta-wīhsini	*she/he will eat*
3's	ta-wīhsiniwan	*his/her _____will eat*
1P	nika-wīhsinimin	*we (ex) will eat*
21	kika-wīhsinimin	*we (in) will eat*
2P	kika-wīhsinim	*you all will eat*
3P	ta-wīhsiniwak	*they will eat*
3'P	ta-wīhsiniwah	*his/her _____s will eat*

V-AI Indicative Aspect (going to)

tōtam – *she/he does so*

1S	niwī-tōtam	*I am going to do so*
2S	kiwī-tōtam	*you are going to do so*
3S	wī-tōtam	*she/he is going to do so*
3's	wī-tōtamōn	*his/her _____is going to do so*
1P	niwī-tōtāmin	*we (ex) are going to do so*
21	kiwī-tōtāmin	*we (in) are going to do so*
2P	kiwī-tōtām	*you all are going to do so*
3P	wī-tōtamōk	*they are going to do so*
3'P	wī-tōtamōh	*his/her _____s are going to do so*

POLARITY OR YES/NO QUESTIONS

You will remember from Chapter 10 that polarity questions are those that may be answered with a *yes* or *no*. They are formed by placing the verb in question at the beginning of the sentence and placing the question indicator *na* after the verb or in the *second position* of a sentence. Remember: the indicator *na* is used in yes/no questions only in the indicative mode.

Anohkī.	*She/he is working.*	statement
Anohkī na?	*Is she/he working?*	yes/no question
Āša na kikī-anohkī?	*Did you work already?*	

The following sentences contain AI verbs in the indicative mode.

Nikawac. *or* Nikīhkac.	*I am cold.*
Kikawac na? *or* Kikīhkac na?	*Are you cold?*
Kawaci. *or* Kīhkaci.	*She/he is cold.*
Nitayēhkos. *(in rapid speech, N'tayēhkos.)*	*I am tired.*
Kikī-ayēhkos na?	*Were you tired?*
Nitāhkos. *(in rapid speech, N'tāhkos.)*	*I am sick.*
Nikišis. *(in rapid speech, N'kišis.)*	*I am hot/fevered.*
Kišiso na oškinīkīns?	*Is the little boy hot/fevered?*
Nimihsēyak kī-āhkosiwak.	*My older sisters were sick.*

Negative Indicative Mode

Like the II verbs, the AI verbs can be put in the negative indicative mode. This mode is the opposite of the indicative mode. The verb uses the particle *kāwīn* "no/not" before the verb, and a negative suffix (*-hsī, -sī, -nsī*) is attached after the verb and before the personal suffix. *Kāwīn* is usually collapsed to *kān*.

No.	Particle	Personal prefix	Verb	Negative suffix	Personal suffix	Translation
V-AI Negative Indicative Mode						
1s	kāwīn	ni-		-hsī		*I'm not…*
2s	kāwīn	ki-		-hsī		*You're not…*
3s	kāwīn			-hsī		*She/he is not…*
3's	kāwīn			-hsī	-wan	*His/her _____ is not…*
1P	kāwīn	ni-		-hsī	-min	*We (ex) are not…*
21	kāwīn	ki-		-hsī	-min	*We (in) are not…*
2P	kāwīn	ki-		-hsī	-m	*You all are not…*
3P	kāwīn			-hsī	-wak	*They are not…*
3'P	kāwīn			-hsī	-wah	*His/her ____s are not…*

Note: The hyphens indicate that the elements are attached to one another.

The 3rd person (3's, 3P, 3'P) suffixes after a consonant are *-ōn*, *-ōk*, and *-ōh*, but when adding a negative suffix, the 3's suffix is *-wan*, the 3P suffix is *-wak*, and the 3'P suffix is *-wah*. This mode can also take the various tenses/aspect pre-verbs, which are attached after the personal prefix and before the verb (examples are given later in this section).

All AI verbs take this pattern, but as with the indicative mode there are a few rules that apply: the connector *-t-* rule applies to the 1st and 2nd persons in the present tense *only*; for verbs that end in short vowels, the vowel does *not* get deleted; and verbs that end in vowels and consonants take different negative suffixes. The rules that apply for attaching negative suffixes are:

1. When a verb ends in a vowel (long and short), the negative suffix is *-hsī*

pāhpi	*she/he is laughing*
kāwīn pāhpi**hsī**	*she/he is not laughing*

2. When a verb ends in -hšin, the negative suffix is -sī

takohšin	*she/he is arriving*
kāwīn takohšin**sī**	*she/he is not arriving*

3. When a verb ends in *-am*, delete the *m* and add *-nsī*

sākaham	*she/he is going out*
kāwīn sākaha**nsī**	*she/he is not going out*

The following tables give examples of AI verbs in the negative indicative mode in various tenses/aspect. The bare verb *nipā* "she/he is sleeping" fits into the basic pattern.

V-AI Negative Indicative Past Tense

nipā – *she/he is sleeping*

1S	kāwīn nikī-nipāhsī	*I am not sleeping*
2S	kāwīn kikī-nipāhsī	*you are not sleeping*
3S	kāwīn kī-nipāhsī	*she/he is not sleeping*
3's	kāwīn kī-nipāhsīwan	*his/her ___ is not sleeping*
1P	kāwīn nikī-nipāhsīmin	*we (ex) are not sleeping*
21	kāwīn kikī-nipāhsīmin	*we (in) are not sleeping*
2P	kāwīn kikī-nipāhsīm	*you all are not sleeping*
3P	kāwīn kī-nipāhsīwak	*they are not sleeping*
3'P	kāwīn kī-nipāhsīwah	*his/her ___s are not sleeping*

For the bare verb *cīhkēntam* "she/he is happy," the final consonant (*m*) is deleted when the negative suffix is attached.

V-AI Negative Indicative Future Definite Tense

cīhkēntam – *she/he is happy*

1s	kāwīn nika-cīhkēntansī	*I will not be happy*
2s	kāwīn kika-cīhkēntansī	*you will not be happy*
3s	kāwīn ta-cīhkēntansī	*she/he will not be happy*
3's	kāwīn ta-cīhkēntansīwan	*his/her ___ will not be happy*
1P	kāwīn nika-cīhkēntansīmin	*we (ex) will not be happy*
21	kāwīn kika-cīhkēntansīmin	*we (in) will not be happy*
2P	kāwīn kika-cīhkēntansīm	*you all will not be happy*
3P	kāwīn ta-cīhkēntansīwak	*they will not be happy*
3'P	kāwīn ta-cīhkēntansīwah	*his/her ___s will not be happy*

Here are a few examples of sentences in the negative indicative mode:

Kāwīn ayapihsī mēkwā.	*She/he is not at home right now.*
Kāwīn anohkīhsīwak nōnkom.	*They are not working today.*
Kāwīn nicīhkēntansī nōnkom.	*I'm not happy today.*

For extra practise, see the Chapter 12 Exercises on pages 166–167.

CHAPTER

· · · · · · · · · · ·

13

Objectives

- Animate intransitive verbs (V-AI), continued
- Subjunctive mode
- Negative subjunctive mode

Dialogues

1. Ānīn ēšinihkāsowan?   *What is your name?*
   Lynn nitišinihkās.   *My name is Lynn.*
   Ānīn ēntōtaman?   *What are you doing?*
   Kān ninipāhsī, nitōtamin.   *I'm not sleeping, I'm playing.*

2. Kī-kīwē na?   *Did she/he go home?*
   Kāwīn kī-kīwēhsī.   *She/he did not go home.*
   Ānahpī kē-kīwēt?   *When will she/he go home?*
   Kān nikihkēntansīn.   *I don't know.*

3. Ānti ēšāt kipāpā?   *Where did your dad go?*
   Kān nipāpā kī-išāhsī atāwēwikamikōnk. *My dad did not go to the store.*
   Cīhkēntamok na?   *Are they happy?*
   Kān cīhkēntansīwak.   *They're not happy.*

Vocabulary

Anamihcikē.	*She/he is reading.*	Kīwē.	*She/he is going home.*
Nakamo.	*She/he is singing.*	Kīkito.	*She/he is speaking.*
Sākaham.	*She/he is going outside.*	Nihšitotam.	*She/he is understanding.*
Takohšin.	*She/he is arriving.*	Āhkosi.	*She/he is sick.*
Išinihkāso.	*She/he is called.*	Ayā.	*She/he is there.*
Nipā.	*She/he is sleeping.*	Otamino.	*She/he is playing.*
Tōtam.	*She/he does so.*	Wīhsini.	*She/he is eating.*
Išā.	*She/he goes.*	Pāhpi.	*She/he is laughing.*
Ayapi.	*She/he is at home.*	Pankihšin.	*She/he is falling.*
Cīhkēntam.	*She/he is happy.*	Mawi.	*She/he is crying.*

Animate Intransitive Verbs (V-AI), continued

Chapter 12 introduced animate intransitive verbs, or V-AI. In this chapter, we continue learning about animate intransitive verbs, focusing on the subjunctive and negative subjunctive modes and exploring a variety of paradigms to compare present tense, past tense, future definite tense, and aspect.

Subjunctive Mode

The subjunctive mode for AI verbs is similar to the subjunctive mode for II verbs (discussed in Chapter 11). It indicates subordination and is considered less "factual" than the indicative mode. It is used to ask *supplementary questions* beginning with interrogative pronouns or conjunctional particles such as *ānti* "where," *ānīn* "how/what," *ānīhšwīn* "why," *ānahpī* "when," *awēnēn* "who (sg)," *awēnēnak* "who (pl)," *wēkonēn* "what (sg)," and *wēkonēnan* "what (pl)." The subjunctive mode is also used in subordinate clauses.

AI verbs in the subjunctive mode require personal affixes that are different from the indicative mode personal affixes. In the indicative mode, the person may be indicated by a prefix, a suffix, or both. In the subjunctive mode, persons are indicated only by personal *suffixes*. This comparison can be seen in the table below. (You will notice that the indicative affixes are those learned in Chapter 12.) As you can see in the table, all animate intransitive verbs in the indicative and subjunctive forms can have nine possible subjects carrying out the action.

No.	Subject	Indicative personal affix	Subjunctive personal suffix
1s	*I*	ni-(verb)	(verb)-yān
2s	*you*	ki-(verb)	(verb)-yan
3s	*she/he*	(bare verb)	(verb)-t
3's	*his/her ___*	(verb) -wan	(verb)-nit
1P	*we* (ex)	ni-(verb)-min	(verb)-yānk
21	*we* (in)	ki-(verb)-min	(verb)-yank
2P	*you all*	ki-(verb)-m	(verb)-yēk
3P	*they*	(verb)-wak	(verb)-wāt
3'P	*his/her ___s*	(verb)-wah	(verb)-nit

Again, V-AI are listed in the 3rd person singular or bare verb form in the present tense of the indicative mode, as in the following examples:

anamihcikē	*she/he is reading*	nakamo	*she/he is singing*
sākaham	*she/he is going outside*	takohšin	*she/he is arriving*

The basic subjunctive mode conjugation paradigms for V-AI are as follows. The particle *kīšpin* "if" is usually used with a verb in the subjunctive mode.

V-AI Subjunctive Mode		ending in vowels -a, -ā, -i, -ī, or -e	ending in -o or -ō	ending in -am or -hšin
1s	*(if) I...*	(kīšpin) -yān	(kīšpin) -wān	(kīšpin) -ān
2s	*(if) you...*	(kīšpin) -yan	(kīšpin) -wan	(kīšpin) -an
3s	*(if) she/he...*	(kīšpin) -t	(kīšpin) -t	(kīšpin) -nk
3's	*(if) his/her ___...*	(kīšpin) -nit	(kīšpin) -nit	(kīšpin) -init
1P	*(if) we* (ex)...	(kīšpin) -yānk	(kīšpin) -wānk	(kīšpin) -ānk
21	*(if) we* (in)...	(kīšpin) -yank	(kīšpin) -wank	(kīšpin) -ank
2P	*(if) you all...*	(kīšpin) -yēk	(kīšpin) -wēk	(kīšpin) -ēk
3P	*(if) they...*	(kīšpin) -wāt	(kīšpin) -wāt	(kīšpin) -owāt / -iwāt
3'P	*(if) his/her ___s...*	(kīšpin) -nit	(kīšpin) -nit	(kīšpin) -init

The following are examples of V-AI in the present tense of the subjunctive mode, following the rules from the paradigm above.

V-AI Subjunctive Present Tense

kīwē – *she/he is going home*

1s	(kīšpin) kīwē**yān**	*(if) I go home...*
2s	(kīšpin) kīwē**yan**	*(if) you go home...*
3s	(kīšpin) kīwē**t**	*(if) she/he goes home...*
3's	(kīšpin) kīwē**nit**	*(if) his/her _____ goes home...*
1P	(kīšpin) kīwē**yānk**	*(if) we (ex) go home...*
21	(kīšpin) kīwē**yank**	*(if) we (in) go home...*
2P	(kīšpin) kīwē**yēk**	*(if) you all go home...*
3P	(kīšpin) kīwē**wāt**	*(if) they go home...*
3'P	(kīšpin) kīwē**nit**	*(if) his/her _____s go home...*

kīkito – *she/he is talking/speaking*

1s	(kīšpin) kīkito**wān**	*(if) I talk/speak...*
2s	(kīšpin) kīkito**wan**	*(if) you talk/speak...*
3s	(kīšpin) kīkito**t**	*(if) she/he talks/speaks...*
3's	(kīšpin) kīkito**nit**	*(if) his/her _____ talks/speaks...*
1P	(kīšpin) kīkito**wānk**	*(if) we (ex) talk/speak...*
21	(kīšpin) kīkito**wank**	*(if) we (in) talk/speak...*
2P	(kīšpin) kīkito**wēk**	*(if) you all talk/speak...*
3P	(kīšpin) kīkito**wāt**	*(if) they talk/speak...*
3'P	(kīšpin) kīkito**nit**	*(if) his/her _____s talk/speak...*

nihšitotam – *she/he understands*

1s	(kīšpin) nihšitotam**ān**	*(if) I understand...*
2s	(kīšpin) nihšitotam**an**	*(if) you understand...*
3s	(kīšpin) nihšitota**nk***	*(if) she/he understands...*
3's	(kīšpin) nihšitotam**init**	*(if) his/her _____ understands...*
1P	(kīšpin) nihšitotam**ānk**	*(if) we (ex) understand...*
21	(kīšpin) nihšitotam**ank**	*(if) we (in) understand...*
2P	(kīšpin) nihšitotam**ēk**†	*(if) you all understand...*
3P	(kīšpin) nihšitotam**owāt**‡	*(if) they understand...*
3'P	(kīšpin) nihšitotam**init**	*(if) his/her _____s understand...*

---

* Notice that the personal suffixes for 3s V-AI ending in *-am* or *-hšin* differ from the personal suffix for verbs ending in vowels.

† The personal suffix for 2P is *-owēk* but gets collapsed to *-ēk*.

‡ Notice 3P also takes a slightly different personal suffix for V-AI ending in *-am* or *-hšin*.

pankihšin – *she/he is falling*

1s	(kīšpin) pankihšin**ān**	*(if) I fall...*
2s	(kīšpin) pankihšin**an**	*(if) you fall...*
3s	(kīšpin) pankihšin**k**	*(if) she/he falls...*
3's	(kīšpin) pankihšin**init**	*(if) his/her____ falls...*
1P	(kīšpin) pankihšin**ānk**	*(if) we (ex) fall...*
21	(kīšpin) pankihšin**ank**	*(if) we (in) fall...*
2P	(kīšpin) pankihšin**ēk**	*(if) you all fall...*
3P	(kīšpin) pankihšin**iwāt**	*(if) they fall...*
3'P	(kīšpin) pankihšin**init**	*(if) his/her ___s fall...*

Here are a few examples of sentences in the subjunctive mode.

Ānahpī kīwēyan?	*When are you going home?*
Ānti ēyāt kimāmā?	*Where is your mother at?*
Kīšpin āhkosiyān, nika-ayap.	*If I'm sick, I'll stay home.*
Ānīn ēntōtaman?	*What are you doing?*

INITIAL CHANGE

Some but not all V-AI go through an initial change in the subjunctive mode, as shown in the second example in the sentences above, *Ānti ēyāt kimāmā?*, where *ayā* changes to *ēyāt*.

An **initial change** occurs when the verb in the indicative mode either begins with a short vowel or contains the short vowels -*a* or -*i* in the first syllable. In these cases, the short vowel changes to the long vowel *ē* for the subjective mode in the present tense. For some indicative verbs that begin in the short vowel -*o*, the vowel changes to *wē*-, only in the present tense of the subjunctive mode (supplementary questions).

Some verbs beginning with the short vowel *a* → *ē*

Present:	**ayā**	*she/he is (there)*	indicative mode
	Ānti **ēyāt?**	*Where is she/he at?*	subjunctive mode (supplementary question)
Past:	kī-**ayā**	*she/he was (there)*	indicative mode
	Ānti kā-**ayāt?**	*Where was she/he at?*	subjunctive mode (supplementary question)

Some verbs beginning with the short vowel *i* → *ē*

Present:	išinihkāso	*his/her name is...*	indicative mode
	Ānīn ēšinihkāsot?	*What is his/her name?*	subjunctive mode
			(supplementary question)
Past:	kī-išinihkāso	*she/he was named*	indicative mode
	Ānīn kā-išinihkāsot?	*What was his/her name?*	subjunctive mode
			(supplementary question)

Some verbs containing the short vowel *-a* in the first syllable: *(C)a → (C)ē*

Present:	takohšin	*she/he is arriving*	indicative mode
	Ānahpī tēhkohšink?	*When does she/he arrive?*	subjunctive mode
Past:	kī-takohšin	*she/he arrived*	indicative mode
	Ānahpī kā-takohšink?	*When did she/he arrive?*	subjunctive mode

Some verbs containing the short vowel *-i* in the first syllable: *(C)i → (C)ē*

Present:	nipā	*she/he is sleeping*	indicative mode
	Awēnēn nēpāt?	*Who is sleeping?*	subjunctive mode
Past:	kī-nipā	*she/he slept*	indicative mode
	Awēnēn kā-nipāt?	*Who slept?*	subjunctive mode

Some verbs beginning with the short vowel *o* → *wē*

Present:	otamino	*she/he is playing*	indicative mode
	Awēnēn wētaminot?	*Who is playing?*	subjunctive mode
Past:	kī-otamino	*she/he played*	indicative mode
	Awēnēn kā-otaminot?	*Who played?*	subjunctive mode

V-AI Subjunctive Present Tense with Initial Change

anohkī – she/he is working

1s	(kīšpin) ēnohkīyān	*(if) I work...*
2s	(kīšpin) ēnohkīyan	*(if) you work...*
3s	(kīšpin) ēnohkīt	*(if) she/he works...*
3's	(kīšpin) ēnohkīnit	*(if) his/her____ works...*
1P	(kīšpin) ēnohkīyānk	*(if) we (ex) work...*
21	(kīšpin) ēnohkīyank	*(if) we (in) work...*
2P	(kīšpin) ēnohkīyēk	*(if) you all work...*
3P	(kīšpin) ēnohkīwāt	*(if) they work...*
3'P	(kīšpin) ēnohkīnit	*(if) his/her ___s work...*

In another type of initial change, in some indicative verbs that begin in *tō-*, the prefix *ēn-* is attached to the front of the verb, but only in the present tense of the subjunctive mode.

Some verbs beginning with *tō-*: *ēn-* + V

Present:	**tō**tam	*she/he does so*	indicative mode
	Ānīn **ēn**tōtank?	*What is she/he doing?*	subjunctive mode
Past:	kī-**tō**tam	*she/he did so*	indicative mode
	Ānīn kā-**tō**tank?	*What did she/he do?*	subjunctive mode

The verb *tā* "she/he resides (there)" or "his/her home" always takes the prefix *ēn-* and is used with the tenses and aspect.

Present:	**tā**	*she/he resides (there)*	indicative mode
	Ānti **ēn**tāt?	*Where is she/he residing?*	subjunctive mode
Past:	Āntī kā-**ēn**tāt?	*Where was his/her home?*	subjunctive mode

This verb can be put in the nine persons and refers to residence or home as in the following:

1s	ēntāyān	*my residence/home*
2s	ēntāyan	*your residence/home*
3s	ēntāt	*his/her residence/home*
3's	ēntānit	*his/her _____ residence(s)/home(s)*
1P	ēntāyānk	*our (ex) residence/home*
21	ēntāyank	*our (in) residence/home*
2P	ēntāyēk	*your (pl) residence/home*
3P	ēntāwāt	*their residence/home*
3'P	ēntānit	*his/her _____s residence(s)/home(s)*

TENSE AND ASPECT

Like the subjunctive mode for inanimate intransitive verbs (V-II) (discussed in Chapter 11), in the subjunctive mode for animate intransitive verbs (V-AI) the tense and aspect pre-verbs go through an initial change.

Indicative →	**Subjunctive mode (V-AI)**
present	no pre-verb
past	kī- → kā-
future definite (will)	ka-, ta- → kē-
aspect (going to)	wī- → wā-

The following charts are examples of V-AI in the subjunctive mode and in the tenses and aspect.

V-AI Subjunctive Past Tense

kīwē – she/he goes home

1S	(kīšpin) **kā**-kīwē*yān*	*(if) I went home...*
2S	(kīšpin) **kā**-kīwē*yan*	*(if) you went home...*
3S	(kīšpin) **kā**-kīwē*t*	*(if) she/he went home...*
3'S	(kīšpin) **kā**-kīwē*nit*	*(if) his/her ____ went home...*
1P	(kīšpin) **kā**-kīwē*yānk*	*(if) we (ex) went home...*
21	(kīšpin) **kā**-kīwē*yank*	*(if) we (in) went home...*
2P	(kīšpin) **kā**-kīwē*yēk*	*(if) you all went home...*
3P	(kīšpin) **kā**-kīwē*wāt*	*(if) they went home...*
3'P	(kīšpin) **kā**-kīwē*nit*	*(if) his/her ____s went home...*

V-AI Subjunctive Future Definite Tense

kīkito – she/he is talking/speaking

1S	(kīšpin) **kē**-kīkito*wān*	*(if) I will talk/speak...*
2S	(kīšpin) **kē**-kīkito*wan*	*(if) you will talk/speak...*
3S	(kīšpin) **kē**-kīkito*t*	*(if) she/he will talk/speak...*
3'S	(kīšpin) **kē**-kīkito*nit*	*(if) his/her ____ will talk/speak...*
1P	(kīšpin) **kē**-kīkito*wānk*	*(if) we (ex) will talk/speak...*
21	(kīšpin) **kē**-kīkito*wank*	*(if) we (in) will talk/speak...*
2P	(kīšpin) **kē**-kīkito*wēk*	*(if) you all will talk/speak...*
3P	(kīšpin) **kē**-kīkito*wāt*	*(if) they will talk/speak...*
3'P	(kīšpin) **kē**-kīkito*nit*	*(if) his/her ____s will talk/speak...*

V-AI Subjunctive Aspect

nihšitotam – she/he understands

1S	(kīšpin) **wā**-nihšitotam*ān*	*(if) I am going to understand...*
2S	(kīšpin) **wā**-nihšitotam*an*	*(if) you are going to understand...*
3S	(kīšpin) **wā**-nihšitota*nk*	*(if) she/he is going to understand...*
3'S	(kīšpin) **wā**-nihšitotam*init*	*(if) his/her ____ is going to understand...*
1P	(kīšpin) **wā**-nihšitotam*ānk*	*(if) we (ex) are going to understand...*
21	(kīšpin) **wā**-nihšitotam*ank*	*(if) we (in) are going to understand...*
2P	(kīšpin) **wā**-nihšitotam*ēk*	*(if) you all are going to understand...*
3P	(kīšpin) **wā**-nihšitotam*owāt*	*(if) they are going to understand...*
3'P	(kīšpin) **wā**-nihšitotam*init*	*(if) his/her ____s are going to understand...*

Here are some examples of V-AI in supplementary questions and subordinate clauses.

Ānīn ēšinihkāsowan?	*What is your name?*
Ānti wīhsiniyānk?	*Where are we (ex) eating?*
Ānahpī kā-išāwāt?	*When did they go (there)?*
Wēkonēn ēntōtaman?	*What are you doing?*
Kāwīn niwī-nīpawihsī ahpī kīkitowān.	*I'm not going to stand when/as I talk/speak.*
Ahpī tēkohšiniwāt, ta-wīhsiniwak na?	*When they arrive, will they eat?*
Kēko pāhpihkēn kīšpin pankihšinān.	*Don't laugh if I fall.*
Kīšpin wētaminot, wīnkē ta-cīhkēntam.	*If she/he plays, she/he will be happy.*
Ānīhšwīn kā-mawit?	*Why did he cry?*
Kīšpin wā-išāyan ōtēnānk, kēnīn nika-išā.	*If you are going to go to town, I too will go (there).*

Negative Subjunctive Mode

The negative subjunctive mode is used to negate a subordinate clause. The particle *kāwīn* is *not* used with this mode. The appropriate negative suffix *-hsi*, *-nsi*, or *-si* (depending on the verb ending) is attached to the end of the verb and before the personal suffix. (As with the subjunctive, the persons are shown in the suffixes.) Interrogative pronouns and conjunctional particles are also used with this mode.

V-AI Negative Subjunctive Present Tense

nipā – *she/he is sleeping*

1s	(kīšpin) nēpā**hsi**wān	*(if) I don't sleep...*
2s	(kīšpin) nēpā**hsi**wan	*(if) you don't sleep...*
3s	(kīšpin) nēpā**hsi**k	*(if) she/he doesn't sleep...*
3's	(kīšpin) nēpā**hsi**nik	*(if) his/her ____ doesn't sleep...*
1P	(kīšpin) nēpā**hsi**wānk	*(if) we (ex) don't sleep...*
21	(kīšpin) nēpā**hsi**wank	*(if) we (in) don't sleep...*
2P	(kīšpin) nēpā**hsi**wēk	*(if) you all don't sleep...*
3P	(kīšpin) nēpā**hsi**kwā	*(if) they don't sleep...*
3'P	(kīšpin) nēpā**hsi**nik	*(if) his/her ____s don't sleep...*

All V-AIs ending in vowels will take *-hsi*, as in the example above (*nipā* – she/he is sleeping). For V-AIs that end in *-am*, the "m" is deleted and the negative suffix *-nsi* is added. V-AIs ending in *-hšin* take the negative suffix *-si*, just like the negative indicative; the only difference in the negative subjunctive is that the suffixes *-hsi*, *-nsi* and *-si* end in a short vowel (*-i*) and the negative indicative suffixes *-hsī*, *-nsī*, and *-sī* end in a long vowel (*-ī*).

Kīšpin ēntōta**nsi**wan, nika-tōtam.   *If you don't do so/it, I will do so/it.*
(verb is *tōtam* "she/he does so/it")

Ānīhšwīn kā-takohšin**si**yan?   *Why didn't you arrive?*
(verb is *takohšin* "she/he is arriving")

The subjunctive mode can also be used in negative statements when the pre-verb *ēkā-* is used. When using *ēkā-*, the negative suffix is not required, and the basic subjunctive personal suffixes are attached.

Negative Subjunctive Using ēkā- and the Subjunctive Personal Suffixes

1s	**ēkā**-anohkīy*ān*	*I did not work*
2s	**ēkā**-anohkīy*an*	*you did not work*
3s	**ēkā**-anohkī*t*	*she/he did not work*
3's	**ēkā**-anohkī*nit*	*his/her _____ did not work*
1P	**ēkā**-anohkīy*ānk*	*we (ex) did not work*
21	**ēkā**-anohkīy*ank*	*we (in) did not work*
2P	**ēkā**-anohkīy*ēk*	*you all did not work*
3P	**ēkā**-anohkīw*āt*	*they did not work*
3'P	**ēkā**-anohkī*nit*	*his/her _____s did not work*

For extra practise, see the Chapter 13 Exercises on pages 168–169.

CHAPTER

14

Objectives

- Introduction to transitive verbs
- Transitive animate verbs (V-TA)
- Imperative and negative imperative modes
- Indicative mode
- Negative indicative mode

Dialogues

1. Awēnēn kā-pīnāt?
   Okī-pīnān otānihsan.

   Who did she/he bring?
   She/he brought his/her daughter.

2. Kikihkēnim na?
   Kāwin, kān nikihkēnimāhsī.

   Do you know her?
   No, I don't know her.

3. Pīš pōsīns!
   Kēko pīnāhkēn awē animohš.

   Bring the cat!
   Don't bring that dog.

4. Kikī-nōntawāk na šīhšīpak?
   Mīnankē, nikī-nōntawāk.

   Did you hear ducks?
   Yes, I heard them.

5. Wāpam awē kiniw!
   Kān nikī-wāpamāhsī, nikī-wāpamā pinēhsī tahs.

   (You) see that eagle!
   I didn't see it, but I saw a bird.

Vocabulary

Wāpam.	*(You) see him/her/it.*	Nōntaw.	*(You) hear him/her/it.*
Amo.	*(You) eat it* (NA).	Ayāw.	*(You) have him/her/it.*
Pīš.	*(You) bring him/her/it.*	Kihkēnim.	*(You) know him/her/it.*
Wīcih.	*(You) help him/her/it.*	Antotaw.	*(You) listen to him/her/it.*
Ahsam.	*(You) feed him/her/it.*	Pīh.	*(You) wait for him/her/it.*

Introduction to Transitive Verbs

You have already been introduced to the intransitive verbs V-II (inanimate intransitive) and V-AI (animate intransitive) in Saulteaux, and over the next four chapters we will look at the transitive verbs, V-TA (transitive animate) and V-TI (transitive inanimate).

The word *transitive* denotes that an action of a sentence is transferred *from* the subject *to* someone or something, the object of the sentence. Transitive verbs contain *both* a *subject* and an *object* and are used with *direct objects*. Just to review, in Saulteaux it's not only important to know whether a verb is **transitive** or **intransitive**; it's also important to know whether the verb is **animate** or **inanimate**.

When the verb changes form according to the subject or the object of a sentence, that change is referred to as **verb agreement**. This means the form of the verb varies depending on who is *doing* the action and who or what is *receiving* the action (object). With the intransitive verbs we've already seen, there was no object receiving the action. The forms still displayed animacy and inanimacy, but it was that of the subject performing the action, as in the following examples:

wīhsini	*she/he is eating*	(intransitive)
otamwān	*she/he eats it* (NA)	(transitive animate)
omīcin	*she/he eats it* (NI)	(transitive inanimate)

With transitive verbs, however, the form of the verb reflects not only the animacy of the *subject*, but also whether the *object* is animate or inanimate. In general, transitive verbs have two forms, one used with animate objects and one used with inanimate objects. The following sentences show that the verb agrees not only with the subject but also with the object.

Nitayān masinahikan.	*I have a book.*
Kitayān na masinahikan?	*Do you have a book?*
Mary otayān masinahikan.	*Mary has a book.*
Mary okosihsan otayāni masinahikan.	*Mary's son has a book.*

In the examples above, the subjects are animate (I, you, Mary, and Mary's son). The object *masinahikan* "a book" is an inanimate noun, and therefore the verb form is transitive inanimate. Transitive inanimate verbs will be discussed in more detail in Chapters 16 and 17.

Transitive Animate Verbs (V-TA)

Transitive animate verbs contain an *animate subject* and an *animate object*.

a)	Wāpam	*See him/her/it!*	(command said to one person)
b)	Niwāpamā	*I see him/her/it.*	(statement)

In command a), the animate subject is *you*, and the action (*to see*) transfers to the animate object *him/her/it*. In statement b), the animate subject is *I*, and the action (*seeing*) transfers to the animate object *him/her/it*.

Transitive verbs are used with direct objects, and a V-TA is used with animate direct objects. Verbs must agree in *number* (singular/plural), in *gender* (animate/inanimate), and in *obviation* (singular/plural), as shown in the following examples.

a)	Amo ošaškwēhtō!	*(You) eat the apple!*	(lit., *you eat it the apple*)
b)	Nikī-amwā ošaškwēhtō.	*I ate the apple.*	(lit., *I ate it the apple*)

In example a) above, the animate subject is *you* (sg), and the action (*to eat*) is transferred to the animate direct object *the apple*. In example b), the animate subject is *I*, and the action (*to eat*) is transferred to the animate direct object *the apple*.

a)	Kakwēcim kipāpā!	*Ask your father!*	(lit., *Ask him your father!*)
b)	Niwāpamā nikosihs.	*I see my son.*	(lit., *I see him my son.*)

In command a) above, the animate subject is *you*, and the action (*to ask*) transfers to the direct object *your father*. In statement (b) the animate subject is *I*, and the action (*seeing*) transfers to the direct object *my son*.

Imperative and Negative Imperative Modes

Transitive verbs are listed in the imperative singular (I.S.) *you*. The *imperative mode* is used to issue a command or a suggestion at the time of speaking or in the present. The *negative imperative mode* is used to negate a command or suggestion. As with AI verbs in the imperative mode, the particle *kēko* "don't" is used.

The following tables will illustrate the transitive animate verbs in their six forms: imperative singular (I.S.), imperative plural (I.P.), imperative inclusive (I.I.), negative imperative singular (N.I.S.), negative imperative plural (N.I.P.) and negative imperative inclusive (N.I.I.). In the charts below, the personal suffix is *italicized* and the negative particle and suffix are **bolded**. The long *ā* that precedes the personal suffix in the I.I, N.I.S., N.I.P., and N.I.I. forms and appears ***italicized and bolded*** is the direction marker for V-TAs and is not part of the personal suffix or negative suffix.

V-TA stems ending in consonants *-m, -w, -n, -h*		
I.S.	_____ -m/-w/-n/-h	*(you)...him/her/it*
I.P.	_____ -*ik*	*(you all)...him/her/it*
I.I.	_____ -***ā****tā*	*let's...him/her/it*
N.I.S.	**kēko** _____ -***ā*hkē***n*	*(you) don't ...him/her/it*
N.I.P.	**kēko** _____ -***ā*hkē***k*	*(you all) don't...him/her/it*
N.I.I.	**kēko** _____ -***ā****tā*	*let's not...him/her/it*

wāpam – *see him/her/it*

wāpam	*(you) see him/her/it*
wāpam*ik*	*(you all) see him/her/it*
wāpam***ā****tā*	*let's see him/her/it*
kēko wāpam***ā*hkē***n*	*(you) don't see him/her/it*
kēko wāpam***ā*hkē***k*	*(you all) don't see him/her/it*
kēko wāpam***ā****tā*	*let's not see him/her/it*

For V-TA stems ending in the consonants *-s* or *–š*, the *-s/–š* is dropped and an *-n* is added in the other five forms (I.P. to N.I.I.).

V-TA stems ending in the consonants *-s* and *-š*		
I.S.	_____ -s/-š	*(you)...him/her/it*
I.P.	_____ -s/-š → *nik*	*(you all)...him/her/it*
I.I.	_____ -s/-š → *n****ā****tā*	*let's...him/her/it*
N.I.S.	**kēko** _____ -s/-š → *n****ā*hkē***n*	*(you) don't ...him/her/it*
N.I.P.	**kēko** _____ -s/-š → *n****ā*hkē***k*	*(you all) don't...him/her/it*
N.I.I.	**kēko** _____ -s/-š → *n****ā****tā*	*let's not...him/her/it*

pīš – *bring him/her/it*

pīš	*(you) bring him/her/it*
pīnik	*(you all) bring him/her/it*
pīnātā	*let's bring him/her/it*
kēko pīn*āhkē*n	*(you) don't bring him/her/it*
kēko pīn*āhkē*k	*(you all) don't bring him/her/it*
kēko pīnātā	*let's not bring him/her/it*

V-TA stems ending in the vowel *-o*		
I.S.	_____-o	*(you)...him/her/it*
I.P.	_____-o → *wāhk*	*(you all)...him/her/it*
I.I.	_____-o → *wātā*	*let's...him/her/it*
N.I.S.	**kēko** _____-o → *wāhkē*n	*(you) don't...him/her/it*
N.I.P.	**kēko** _____-o → *wāhkē*k	*(you all) don't...him/her/it*
N.I.I.	**kēko** _____-o → *wātā*	*let's not...him/her/it*

amo – *eat it* (NA)

amo	*(you) eat it*
am*wāhk*	*(you all) eat it*
am*wātā*	*let's eat it*
kēko am*wāhkē*n	*(you) don't eat it*
kēko am*wāhkē*k	*(you all) don't eat it*
kēko am*wātā*	*let's not eat it*

Here are some examples of V-TAs in the imperative singular (I.S.):

Wāpam awē animohš.	*See that dog.*
Pīš kimāmā.	*Bring your mother.*
Antotawik okihkinahomākē.	*You all listen to the teacher.*
Kēko ahsamāhkēn awē pōsīns.	*Don't feed that cat.*
Kēko amwāhkēk pahkwēšikan.	*You all don't eat the bannock.*
Wīcih kimihšōmihš.	*Help your grandfather.*

Indicative Mode

A verb in the indicative mode in Saulteaux requires *personal affixes* to express who *is doing* the action or who *is* something. Transitive verbs have a personal prefix for 3rd person singular *she/he*. The indicative personal prefixes in this chapter are: *ni-* "I," *ki-* "you," and *o-* "she/he."

The following tables contain the various V-TA stems in the indicative mode paradigms. The verbs are all in the present tense (tense will be discussed in the next section of this chapter).

V-TA Indicative Mode Paradigm		
1s	ni- (verb) -ā	I...him/her/it
2s	ki- (verb) -ā	you...him/her/it
3s	o- (verb) -ān	she/he...him/her/it
3's	o- (verb) -āni	his/her _____...him/her/it
1P	ni- (verb) -ānān	we (ex)...him/her/it
21	ki- (verb) -ānān	we (in)...him/her/it
2P	ki- (verb) -āwā	you all...him/her/it
3P	o- (verb) -āwān	they...him/her/it
3'P	o- (verb) -āni	his/her _____s ...him/her/it

Note that when a verb begins with a vowel, the connector -t- is inserted in the 1st, 2nd, and 3rd persons, singular and plural, *nit-*, *kit-*, and *ot-*. Also, the V-TA indicative mode paradigm changes slightly for verbs ending in *-s/-š* and *-o*.

The following tables show examples of TA verbs with the various stem endings.

V-TA ending in -m

wāpam – *see him/her/it*

1s	**ni**wāpam*ā*	*I see him/her/it*
2s	**ki**wāpam*ā*	*you see him/her/it*
3s	o**wāpam*ān*	*she/he sees him/her/it*
3's	o**wāpam*āni*	*his/her ____ sees him/her/it*
1P	**ni**wāpam*ānān*	*we (ex) see him/her/it*
21	**ki**wāpam*ānān*	*we (in) see him/her/it*
2P	**ki**wāpam*āwā*	*you all see him/her/it*
3P	o**wāpam*āwān*	*they see him/her/it*
3'P	o**wāpam*āni*	*his/her ____s see him/her/it*

When a TA verb ending in *-s/-š* is conjugated into the nine persons in the indicative mode, the *-s/-š* gets dropped and *-n* is added.

V-TA ending in -s/-š

pīš – *bring him/her/it*

1S	**ni**pīn*ā*	*I bring him/her/it*
2S	**ki**pīn*ā*	*you bring him/her/it*
3S	**o**pīn*ā*n	*she/he brings him/her/it*
3's	**o**pīn*ā***ni**	*his/her ____ brings him/her/it*
1P	**ni**pīn*ā***nān**	*we (ex) bring him/her/it*
21	**ki**pīn*ā***nān**	*we (in) bring him/her/it*
2P	**ki**pīn*ā***wā**	*you all bring him/her/it*
3P	**o**pīn*ā***wān**	*they bring him/her/it*
3'P	**o**pīn*ā***ni**	*his/her ____s bring him/her/it*

For TA verbs that end in an *-o*, the *-o* gets dropped and *-w(ā)* is added, as in the following example. This example also illustrates the connector *-t-* rule for V-TAs that begin with a vowel.

V-TA ending in -o

amo – *eat it* (NA)

1S	**ni**tamw*ā*	*I'm eating it*
2S	**ki**tamw*ā*	*you are eating it*
3S	**o**tamw*ā*n	*she/he is eating it*
3's	**o**tamw*ā***ni**	*his/her ____ is eating it*
1P	**ni**tamw*ā***nān**	*we (ex) are eating it*
21	**ki**tamw*ā***nān**	*we (in) are eating it*
2P	**ki**tamw*ā***wā**	*you all are eating it*
3P	**o**tamw*ā***wān**	*they are eating it*
3'P	**o**tamw*ā***ni**	*his/her ____s are eating it*

Here are a few examples of sentences with TA verbs in the indicative mode:

Ninōntawā pinēhsī.	*I hear a bird.*
Otamwān pahkwēšikanan.	*She is eating bannock.*
Kikihkēnimā na?	*Do you know him/her?*
Owāpamāwān mištatimōn.	*They see a horse.*
Nipīhānān nimāmāyinān.	*We (ex) are waiting for our mother.*

TENSE AND ASPECT

Tense and aspect pre-verbs can also be used with the indicative and negative indicative modes. The standard verb structure for V-TA is as follows:

Personal prefix	Tense/aspect pre-verbs	Pre-verbs	Verb root/stem	Personal suffix
ni(t)- ki(t)- (t)-	kī- (past) ka- (future definite, 1st, 2nd pers) ta- (future definite, 3rd pers) wī- (aspect)			(-ā)

V-TA Indicative Past Tense

wāpam – *see him/her/it*

1S	ni**kī**-wāpam*ā*	*I saw him/her/it*
2S	ki**kī**-wāpam*ā*	*you saw him/her/it*
3S	o**kī**-wāpam*ā*n	*she/he saw him/her/it*
3'S	o**kī**-wāpam*ā*ni	*his/her _____ saw him/her/it*
1P	ni**kī**-wāpam*ā*nān	*we (ex) saw him/her/it*
21	ki**kī**-wāpam*ā*nān	*we (in) saw him/her/it*
2P	ki**kī**-wāpam*ā*wā	*you all saw him/her/it*
3P	o**kī**-wāpam*ā*wān	*they saw him/her/it*
3'P	o**kī**-wāpam*ā*ni	*his/her _____s saw him/her/it*

V-TA Indicative Future Definite Tense

nōntaw – *hear him/her/it*

1S	ni**ka**-nōntaw*ā*	*I will hear him/her/it*
2S	ki**ka**-nōntaw*ā*	*you will hear him/her/it*
3S	o**ta**-nōntaw*ā*n	*she/he will hear him/her/it*
3'S	o**ta**-nōntaw*ā*ni	*his/her _____ will hear him/her/it*
1P	ni**ka**-nōntaw*ā*nān	*we (ex) will hear him/her/it*
21	ki**ka**-nōntaw*ā*nān	*we (in) will hear him/her/it*
2P	ki**ka**-nōntaw*ā*wā	*you all will hear him/her/it*
3P	o**ta**-nōntaw*ā*wān	*they will hear him/her/it*
3'P	o**ta**-nōntaw*ā*ni	*his/her _____s will hear him/her/it*

pīš – *bring him/her/it*

1S	ni**wī**-pīnā	*I am going to bring him/her/it*
2S	ki**wī**-pīnā	*you are going to bring him/her/it*
3S	o**wī**-pīnān	*she/he is going to bring him/her/it*
3's	o**wī**-pīnāni	*his/her _____ is going to bring him/her/it*
1P	ni**wī**-pīnānān	*we (ex) are going to bring him/her/it*
21	ki**wī**-pīnānān	*we (in) are going to bring him/her/it*
2P	ki**wī**-pīnāwā	*you all are going to bring him/her/it*
3P	o**wī**-pīnāwān	*they are going to bring him/her/it*
3'P	o**wī**-pīnāni	*his/her _____s are going to bring him/her/it*

Here are some examples of TA verbs in the standard verb structure:

Niwī-amwā ošaškwēhtō.	*I'm going to eat an apple.*
Kikī-kihkēnim na nimihšōmihšipan?	*Did you know my late grandfather?*
Nicīmēns okī-wāpamān nihsayēhinān.	*My younger sibling saw our older brother.*
Nika-pīhānān okimāhkān.	*We will wait for the chief.*
Ota-kipitināwān mištatimōk.	*They will stop the horses.*
Nōsihs owī-kipitinān opāpāyan.	*My grandchild is going to stop his/her dad.*

Negative Indicative Mode

In the negative indicative mode, the verb is negated by using the negative particle *kāwīn* "no/not" before the verb and attaching a negative suffix to the end of the verb root/stem. The negative suffix for TA verb roots/stems is *-hsī* in 1s, 2s, and 3s and *-hsi* in 3's to 3'P. *Kāwīn* is usually shortened to *kān*.

No.	Particle	Personal Prefix	Verb	Negative suffix	Personal Suffix	Translation
V-TA Negative Indicative Mode						
1s	kāwīn	ni-	-ā	-hsī		*I do not...him/her*
2s	kāwīn	ki-	-ā	-hsī		*you do not...him/her*
3s	kāwīn	o-	-ā	-hsī	-n	*she/he does not...him/her*
3's	kāwīn	o-	-ā	-hsi	-ni	*his/her __ does not...him/her*
1P	kāwīn	ni-	-ā	-hsi	-wānān	*we (ex) do not...him/her*
21	kāwīn	ki-	-ā	-hsi	-wānān	*we (in) do not...him/her*
2P	kāwīn	ki-	-ā	-hsi	-wāwā	*you all do not...him/her*
3P	kāwīn	o-	-ā	-hsi	-wāwān	*they do not...him/her*
3'P	kāwīn	o-	-ā	-hsi	-ni	*his/her ___s do not...him/her*

V-TA ending in **m**

wāpam – *see him/her/it*

1S	**kāwīn** niwāpam*a***hsī**	*I do not see him/her/it*
2S	**kāwīn** kiwāpam*a***hsī**	*you do not see him/her/it*
3S	**kāwīn** owāpam*a***hsī**n	*she/he does not see him/her/it*
3'S	**kāwīn** owāpam*a***hsi**ni	*his/her ____ does not see him/her/it*
1P	**kāwīn** niwāpam*a***hsi**nān	*we (ex) do not see him/her/it*
21	**kāwīn** kiwāpam*a***hsi**nān	*we (in) do not see him/her/it*
2P	**kāwīn** kiwāpam*a***hsi**wā	*you all do not see him/her/it*
3P	**kāwīn** owāpam*a***hsi**wān	*they do not see him/her/it*
3'P	**kāwīn** owāpam*a***hsi**ni	*his/her ____s do not see him/her/it*

For TA verbs that end in *-s/-š* or *-o*, the same rules as noted above apply: *-s/-š* → *-n* and *-o* → *-wā* when the verbs are conjugated into the nine persons.

When using tense or aspect, the position of the pre-verb is similar to all verb modes.

Negative particle	Personal prefix	Tense/aspect pre-verbs	Pre-verbs	Verb root/stem	Negative suffix	Personal suffix
kāwīn (kān)	ni(t)- ki(t)- o(t)-	kī- ka- ta- wī-		(-ā)	-hsī	

Kāwīn niwāpamāhsī omā.	*I don't see him/her here.*
Kāwīn okī-amwāhsīn pāhkāhakwānan.	*She did not eat chicken.*
Kāwīn okihkēnimāhsiwāwān.	*They do not know him.*
Kāwīn nika-wāpamāhsiwānān nihsayē.	*We will not see my older brother.*

For extra practise, see the Chapter 14 Exercises on pages 170–171.

CHAPTER

· · · · · · · · · ·

15

Objectives

- Transitive animate verbs (V-TA), continued
- Subjunctive mode
- Negative subjunctive mode

Dialogues

1. Awēnēn kā-mihkawat?   *Who did you find?*
   Nikī-mihkawā nikosihs.   *I found my son.*

2. Kikī-pīnā na ahsēmā?   *Did you bring tobacco?*
   Nikī-wanīhkē ci-pīnak.   *I forgot to bring it.*

3. Ānīhšwīn wēnci-kī-pīnāhsiwat kišōniyām?   *Why didn't you bring your money?*
   Kīšpin ayāwakipan šōniyā, nitākī-atāwē   *If I had money, I would have brought tobacco.*
       ahsēmā.

4. Awēnēn kā-kanōnat?   *Who did you speak to?*
   Nikī-kanōnā nihsayē.   *I spoke to my older brother.*

5. Awēnēn wīcihāt?   *Who is she/he helping?*
   Owīcihān omāmāyan.   *She/he is helping her mother.*

6. Ānahpī kē-kanōnat?   *When will you speak to him/her?*
   Kīšpin kanōnāhsiwāk nōnkom,   *If I don't speak to him/her today, I will speak to*
       nika-kanōnā wāpank.   *him/her tomorrow.*

Vocabulary

Antonēh.	*(You) look for him/her/it.*	Mīš.	*(You) give it to him/her/it.*
Kanōš.	*(You) call him/her/it.*	Mihkaw.	*(You) find him/her/it.*
Nāškaw.	*(You) fetch him/her/it.*	Kakwēcim.	*(You) ask him/her/it.*
Āpahcih.	*(You) use him/her/it.*		

Transitive Animate Verbs (V-TA), continued

In Chapter 14, you were introduced to transitive animate verbs, or V-TA. In this chapter, we will look at the subjunctive and negative subjunctive modes of this verb type, exploring a variety of paradigms to compare present tense, past tense, future definite tense, and aspect.

Subjunctive Mode

As we've seen with the intransitive verbs, the subjunctive mode is used to ask *supplementary questions* that must be supplemented with an answer. The subjunctive mode is also used in *subordinate clauses*, which must be joined to a main clause to be grammatical.

V-TA in the subjunctive mode require personal affixes that are very different from the indicative mode. The subjunctive mode persons are indicated by personal suffixes, as shown in the following tables.

V-TA Subjunctive Mode			
1s	(kīšpin)	-ak	*(if) I...him/her/it*
2s	(kīšpin)	-at	*(if) you...him/her/it*
3s	(kīšpin)	-āt	*(if) she/he...him/her/it*
3's	(kīšpin)	-ānit	*(if) his/her _____...him/her/it*
1P	(kīšpin)	-ankit	*(if) we (ex)...him/her/it*
21	(kīšpin)	-ankit	*(if) we (in)...him/her/it*
2P	(kīšpin)	-āyēk	*(if) you all...him/her/it*
3P	(kīšpin)	-āwāt	*(if) they...him/her/it*
3'P	(kīšpin)	-ānit	*(if) his/her _____s...him/her/it*

For TA verbs that end in *s/š* or *o*, the same rules that we saw in the indicative mode apply: *s/š* → *n* and *o* → *wā* when the verbs are put in the subjunctive mode.

wāpam – *(you) see him/her/it*

1s	(kīšpin) wāpam**ak**	*(if) I see him/her/it*
2s	(kīšpin) wāpam**at**	*(if) you see him/her/it*
3s	(kīšpin) wāpam**āt**	*(if) she/he sees him/her/it*
3's	(kīšpin) wāpam**ānit**	*(if) his/her ____ sees him/her/it*
1P	(kīšpin) wāpam**ankit**	*(if) we (ex) see him/her/it*
21	(kīšpin) wāpam**ankit**	*(if) we (in) see him/her/it*
2P	(kīšpin) wāpam**āyēk**	*(if) you all see him/her/it*
3P	(kīšpin) wāpam**āwāt**	*(if) they see him/her/it*
3'P	(kīšpin) wāpam**ānit**	*(if) his/her ____s see him/her/it*

Āwēnēn nōntawat?	*Who do you hear?*
Āwēnēn amwāt pahkwēšikanan?	*Who is eating bannock?*
Nika-cīhkēntam **kīšpin pīnat nimāmā**.	*I will be happy **if you bring my mother**.*
Kīšpin wāpamak, mahkwa nika-šēkis.	***If I see a bear**, I will be afraid.*

The first two examples above are supplementary questions, and in each of the last two examples the subordinate clause is bolded.

Tense and aspect pre-verbs can also be attached to the front of the verbs in the subjunctive mode. As mentioned before, the subjunctive mode tense/aspect pre-verbs *differ* from the indicative mode tense/aspect pre-verbs, as shown in the chart below. The vowel in tense/aspect pre-verbs goes through an initial change when used in the subjunctive mode. For a review of this change, see Chapter 13.

present	no pre-verb
past	kā-
future definite (will)	kē-
aspect (going to)	wā-

The following charts are examples of V-TA in the subjunctive mode and in the tenses and aspect.

V-TA Subjunctive Past Tense

antonēh – *(you) look for him/her/it*

1S	(kīspin) **kā**-antonēhak	*(if) I looked for him/her/it...*
2S	(kīspin) **kā**-antonēhat	*(if) you looked for him/her/it...*
3S	(kīspin) **kā**-antonēhāt	*(if) she/he looked for him/her/it...*
3's	(kīspin) **kā**-antonēhānit	*(if) his/her _____ looked for him/her/it...*
1P	(kīspin) **kā**-antonēhankit	*(if) we (ex) looked for him/her/it...*
21	(kīspin) **kā**-antonēhankit	*(if) we (in) looked for him/her/it...*
2P	(kīspin) **kā**-antonēhāyēk	*(if) you all looked for him/her/it...*
3P	(kīspin) **kā**-antonēhāwāt	*(if) they looked for him/her/it...*
3'P	(kīspin) **kā**-antonēhānit	*(if) his/her _____s looked for him/her/it...*

V-TA Subjunctive Future Definite Tense

mīš – *(you) give it to him/her/it*

1S	(kīspin) **kē**-mīnak	*(if) I will give it to him/her/it...*
2S	(kīspin) **kē**-mīnat	*(if) you will give it to him/her/it...*
3S	(kīspin) **kē**-mīnāt	*(if) she/he will give it to him/her/it...*
3's	(kīspin) **kē**-mīnānit	*(if) his/her _____ will give it to him/her/it...*
1P	(kīspin) **kē**-mīnankit	*(if) we (ex) will give it to him/her/it...*
21	(kīspin) **kē**-mīnankit	*(if) we (in) will give it to him/her/it...*
2P	(kīspin) **kē**-mīnāyēk	*(if) you all will give it to him/her/it...*
3P	(kīspin) **kē**-mīnāwāt	*(if) they will give it to him/her/it...*
3'P	(kīspin) **kē**-mīnānit	*(if) his/her _____s will give it to him/her/it...*

V-TA Subjunctive Aspect

mihkaw – *(you) find him/her/it*

1S	(kīspin) **wā**-mihkawak	*(if) I am going to find him/her/it...*
2S	(kīspin) **wā**-mihkawat	*(if) you are going to find him/her/it...*
3S	(kīspin) **wā**-mihkawāt	*(if) she/he is going to find him/her/it...*
3's	(kīspin) **wā**-mihkawānit	*(if) his/her _____ is going to find him/her/it...*
1P	(kīspin) **wā**-mihkawankit	*(if) we (ex) are going to find him/her/it...*
21	(kīspin) **wā**-mihkawankit	*(if) we (in) are going to find him/her/it...*
2P	(kīspin) **wā**-mihkawāyēk	*(if) you all are going to find him/her/it...*
3P	(kīspin) **wā**-mihkawāwāt	*(if) they are going to find him/her/it...*
3'P	(kīspin) **wā**-mihkawānit	*(if) his/her _____s are going to find him/her/it...*

Āwēnēn wā-wāpamāt?	*Who are you going to see?*
Ānahpī kē-antotawāt kipāpāyan?	*When will you listen to your dad?*
Nikā-kanōnā kīspin wāpamak.	*I will speak to him/her if I see him/her.*
Kīspin nakiškawat, kika-anamihkawā na?	*If you meet him/her, will you greet him/her?*

Negative Subjunctive Mode

The negative subjunctive mode is used to negate a subordinate clause. The particle *kāwīn* is *not* used with this mode. The negative suffix *-hsi* is attached to the end of the verb and before the personal suffix. As with the subjunctive, the persons are shown using suffixes. The personal suffixes for the negative subjunctive mode differ from those in the subjunctive mode, as shown in the following table. Interrogative pronouns and conjunctional particles are also used with this mode.

V-TA Negative Subjunctive Mode Paradigm

1s	(kīšpin)	-(ā)**hsi**wāk	*(if) I do not...him/her/it*
2s	(kīšpin)	-(ā)**hsi**wat	*(if) you do not...him/her/it*
3s	(kīšpin)	-(ā)**hsi**īhk	*(if) she/he does not...him/her/it*
3's	(kīšpin)	-(ā)**hsi**nik	*(if) his/her _____ does not...him/her/it*
1P	(kīšpin)	-(ā)**hsi**nit	*(if) we (ex) do not...him/her/it*
21	(kīšpin)	-(ā)**hsi**nit	*(if) we (in) do not...him/her/it*
2P	(kīšpin)	-(ā)**hsi**wāyēk	*(if) you all do not...him/her/it*
3P	(kīšpin)	-(ā)**hsi**yēkwā	*(if) they do not...him/her/it*
3'P	(kīšpin)	-(ā)**hsi**nik	*(if) his/her _____s do not...him/her/it*

V-TA Negative Subjunctive Present Tense

wāpam – *see him/her/it* (remember, the verb root of *wāpam* is *wāpamā*)

1s	(kīšpin) wāpamā**hsi**wān	*(if) I do not see him/her/it*
2s	(kīšpin) wāpamā**hsi**wan	*(if) you do not see him/her/it*
3s	(kīšpin) wāpamā**hsi**k	*(if) she/he does not see him/her/it*
3's	(kīšpin) wāpamā**hsi**nik	*(if) his/her _____ does not see him/her/it*
1P	(kīšpin) wāpamā**hsi**wānk	*(if) we (ex) do not see him/her/it*
21	(kīšpin) wāpamā**hsi**wank	*(if) we (in) do not see him/her/it*
2P	(kīšpin) wāpamā**hsi**wēk	*(if) you all do not see him/her/it*
3P	(kīšpin) wāpamā**hsi**kwā	*(if) they do not see him/her/it*
3'P	(kīšpin) wāpamā**hsi**nik	*(if) his/her _____s do not see him/her/it*

Tense and aspect pre-verbs are also used with the negative subjunctive mode, and they are placed before the verb.

present	no pre-verb
past	kā-
future definite (will)	kē-
aspect (going to)	wā-

The following charts are examples of V-TA in the negative subjunctive mode and in the tenses and aspect.

V-TA Negative Subjunctive Past Tense

nāškaw – *(you) fetch him/her/it*

1s	(kīspin) **kā**-nāškawā**hsi**wān	*(if) I did not fetch him/her/it...*
2s	(kīspin) **kā**-nāškawā**hsi**wan	*(if) you did not fetch him/her/it...*
3s	(kīspin) **kā**-nāškawā**hsi**k	*(if) she/he did not fetch him/her/it...*
3's	(kīspin) **kā**-nāškawā**hsi**nik	*(if) his/her _____ did not fetch him/her/it...*
1P	(kīspin) **kā**-nāškawā**hsi**wānk	*(if) we (ex) did not fetch him/her/it...*
21	(kīspin) **kā**-nāškawā**hsi**wank	*(if) we (in) did not fetch him/her/it...*
2P	(kīspin) **kā**-nāškawā**hsi**wēk	*(if) you all did not fetch him/her/it...*
3P	(kīspin) **kā**-nāškawā**hsi**kwā	*(if) they did not fetch him/her/it...*
3'P	(kīspin) **kā**-nāškawā**hsi**nik	*(if) his/her _____s did not fetch him/her/it...*

V-TA Negative Subjunctive Future Definite Tense

kakwēcim – *(you) ask him/her/it*

1s	(kīspin) **kē**-kakwēcimā**hsi**wān	*(if) I will not ask him/her/it...*
2s	(kīspin) **kē**-kakwēcimā**hsi**wan	*(if) you will not ask him/her/it...*
3s	(kīspin) **kē**-kakwēcimā**hsi**k	*(if) she/he will not ask him/her/it...*
3's	(kīspin) **kē**-kakwēcimā**hsi**nik	*(if) his/her _____ will not ask him/her/it...*
1P	(kīspin) **kē**-kakwēcimā**hsi**wānk	*(if) we (ex) will not ask him/her/it...*
21	(kīspin) **kē**-kakwēcimā**hsi**wank	*(if) we (in) will not ask him/her/it...*
2P	(kīspin) **kē**-kakwēcimā**hsi**wēk	*(if) you all will not ask him/her/it...*
3P	(kīspin) **kē**-kakwēcimā**hsi**kwā	*(if) they will not ask him/her/it...*
3'P	(kīspin) **kē**-kakwēcimā**hsi**nik	*(if) his/her _____s will not ask him/her/it...*

V-TA Negative Subjunctive Aspect

wīcih – *(you) help him/her/it*

1s	(kīspin) **wā**-wīcihā**hsi**wān	*(if) I am not going to help him/her/it...*
2s	(kīspin) **wā**-wīcihā**hsi**wan	*(if) you are not going to help him/her/it...*
3s	(kīspin) **wā**-wīcihā**hsi**k	*(if) she/he is not going to help him/her/it...*
3's	(kīspin) **wā**-wīcihā**hsi**nik	*(if) his/her _____ is not going to help him/her/it...*
1P	(kīspin) **wā**-wīcihā**hsi**wānk	*(if) we (ex) are not going to help him/her/it...*
21	(kīspin) **wā**-wīcihā**hsi**wank	*(if) we (in) are not going to help him/her/it...*
2P	(kīspin) **wā**-wīcihā**hsi**wēk	*(if) you all are not going to help him/her/it...*
3P	(kīspin) **wā**-wīcihā**hsi**kwā	*(if) they are not going to help him/her/it...*
3'P	(kīspin) **wā**-wīcihā**hsi**nik	*(if) his/her _____s are not going to help him/her/it...*

This form can also be negated without using a negative suffix by using the pre-verb *ēkā-* instead and adding the personal suffixes from the subjunctive mode, as in the following table.

Negative Subjunctive Using ēkā- and the Subjunctive Personal Suffixes

wāpam – *see him/her/it*

1S	(kīšpin) **ēkā**-wāpamak	*(if) I do not see him/her/it...*
2S	(kīšpin) **ēkā**-wāpamat	*(if) you do not see him/her/it...*
3S	(kīšpin) **ēkā**-wāpamāt	*(if) she/he does not see him/her/it...*
3'S	(kīšpin) **ēkā**-wāpamānit	*(if) his/her _____ does not see him/her/it...*
1P	(kīšpin) **ēkā**-wāpamankit	*(if) we (ex) do not see him/her/it...*
21	(kīšpin) **ēkā**-wāpamankit	*(if) we (in) do not see him/her/it...*
2P	(kīšpin) **ēkā**-wāpamāyēk	*(if) you all do not see him/her/it...*
3P	(kīšpin) **ēkā**-wāpamāwāt	*(if) they do not see him/her/it...*
3'P	(kīšpin) **ēkā**-wāpamānit	*(if) his/her _____s do not see him/her/it...*

Kīšpin wāpamāhsiwāk nōnkom,
  nika-wāpamā wāpank.
(or using ēkā-)
Kīšpin ēkā-wāpamak nōnkom, nika-wāpamā wāpank.

If I don't see him/her today, *I will see*
  him/her tomorrow.

Kīšpin pāhpihāhsiwat, kān ta-niškātišihsī.   *If you don't laugh at him, he will not be angry/mad.*

For extra practise, see the Chapter 15 Exercises on page 172.

CHAPTER

16

Objectives

- Transitive inanimate verbs (V-TI)
- Imperative and negative imperative modes
- Indicative mode
- Negative indicative mode

Dialogues

1. Wēkonēn nōntaman? *What do you hear?*
   Ninōntān otāpān. *I hear a car.*
   Kān ninōntansīn kēko. *I don't hear anything.*

2. Otayān na minihkwācikan? *Does she/he have a cup?*
   Mīnankē otayān minihkwācikan. *Yes, she/he has a cup.*
   Kāwīn otayāhsīn minihkwācikan. *She/he doesn't have a cup.*

3. Mīcin owē napōp! *(You) eat this soup!*
   Kān ninōntē-mīcihsīn owē napōp. *I don't want to eat this soup.*

4. Kēko pītōhkēn iwē masinahikan! *(You) don't bring that book!*
   Wēkonēn masinahikan ēnantawēntaman? *What book do you want?*

Vocabulary

Wāpantan.	*(You) see it.*	Nōntan.	*(You) hear it.*
Mīcin.	*(You) eat it* (NI).	Ayān.	*(You) have it.*
Pītōn.	*(You) bring it.*	Kihkēntan.	*(You) know it.*

Transitive Inanimate Verbs (V-TI)

The last verbs we will examine are the transitive inanimate verbs (V-TI). Transitive inanimate verbs are listed in the imperative singular (I.S.).

Transitive inanimate verbs contain an *animate subject* and an *inanimate object.*

a) wāpantan   *See it!*
b) niwāpantān   *I see it.*

In command a), the animate subject is *you*, and the action (*to see*) transfers to the inanimate object *it*. In statement b), the animate subject is *I*, and the action (*seeing*) transfers to the inanimate object *it*.

Transitive verbs transfer the action to direct objects, and transitive *inanimate* verbs are used with *inanimate* direct objects. Verbs must agree in number (singular/plural), in gender (animate/inanimate), and obviation (singular/plural), as in the following examples:

a) Kipahan iškwāntēm!   *Close the door!* (lit., *Close it, the door!*)
b) Niwāpantān otāpān.   *I see a/the car.* (lit., *I see it, a/the car.*)

In command a), the animate subject is *you*, and the action (*to close*) transfers to the direct object *the door*. In statement b), the animate subject is *I*, and the action (*seeing*) transfers to the direct object *a car*.

Imperative and Negative Imperative Modes

The imperative mode issues a command or a suggestion at the time of speaking or in the present, and the negative imperative mode is used to negate a command or suggestion. The particle *kēko* "don't" is used with this mode.

The following tables will illustrate the transitive inanimate verbs in their six forms; imperative singular (I.S.), imperative plural (I.P.), imperative inclusive (I.I.), negative imperative singular (N.I.S.), negative imperative plural (N.I.P.) and negative imperative inclusive (N.I.I.). The personal suffix is *italicized* and the negative particle and suffix are **bolded**.

V-TI stems with the final short vowel -i or the long vowel -ō		
I.S.	_____-*n*	*(you)...it*
I.P.	_____-*k*	*(you all)...it*
I.I.	_____-*tā*	*let's...it*
N.I.S.	**kēko** _____-**hkē***n*	*(you) don't...it*
N.I.P.	**kēko** _____-**hkē***k*	*(you all) don't...it*
N.I.I.	**kēko** _____-*tā*	*let's not...it*

In the following example, *mīci-* is the verb stem.

mīcin – *eat it* (NI)

mīci*n*	*(you) eat it*
mīci*k*	*(you all) eat it*
mīci*tā*	*let's eat it*
kēko mīci**hkē***n*	*(you) don't eat it*
kēko mīci**hkē***k*	*(you all) don't eat it*
kēko mīci*tā*	*let's not eat it*

In this example, *pītō-* is the verb stem.

pītōn – *bring it* (NI)

pītō*n*	*(you) bring it*
pītō*k*	*(you all) bring it*
pītō*tā*	*let's bring it*
kēko pītō**hkē***n*	*(you) don't bring it*
kēko pītō**hkē***k*	*(you all) don't bring it*
kēko pītō*tā*	*let's not bring it*

V-TI stems with the final short vowel -a		
I.S.	_____-n	*(you)...it*
I.P.	_____-mok	*(you all)...it*
I.I.	_____-ntā	*let's...it*
N.I.S.	**kēko _____-nkē**n	*(you) don't...it*
N.I.P.	**kēko _____-nkē**k	*(you all) don't...it*
N.I.I.	**kēko _____-ntā**	*let's not...it*

In this example, *wāpanta-* is the verb stem.

wāpantan – *see it*

wāpanta*n*	*(you) see it*
wāpanta*mok*	*(you all) see it*
wāpanta*ntā*	*let's see it*
kēko wāpanta**nkē***n*	*(you) don't see it*
kēko wāpanta**nkē***k*	*(you all) don't see it*
kēko wāpanta*ntā*	*let's not see it*

Here are some examples of V-TIs in the imperative singular (I.S.):

Wāpantan iwē otāpān.	*See that car.*
Pītōn kimahkisin.	*Bring your shoe.*
Kipahan iškwāntēm.	*Close the door.*
Kēko mīcihkēn owē wāwan.	*Don't eat this egg.*
Kēko āpahcitōhkēn nitōtāpān.	*Don't use my car. (sg)*
Nanāhitōn iškwāntēm.	*Fix the door.*

Indicative Mode

As with the other types of verbs, the indicative is used for statements and yes/no questions with TI verbs. The same personal pronouns you have already been introduced to are also used with these verbs. The indicative personal prefixes presented in this chapter are *ni-* "I," *ki-* "you," and *o-* "she/he." Remember, transitive verbs have a personal prefix for 3rd person singular "she/he."

The following tables contain the basic paradigm for the various V-TI stems in the indicative mode. The verbs are all in the present tense (tense will be presented in the next section).

V-TI Indicative Mode Paradigm

1S	**ni**- (verb) -**n**	I...it
2S	**ki**- (verb) -**n**	you...it
3S	**o**- (verb) -**n**	she/he...it
3'S	**o**- (verb) -**ni**	his/her _____...it
1P	**ni**- (verb) -**min**	we (ex)...it
21	**ki**- (verb) -**min**	we (in)...it
2P	**ki**- (verb) -**m**	you all...it
3P	**o**- (verb) -**nǎwǎ**	they...it
3'P	**o**- (verb) -**ni**	his/her _____s...it

All TI verbs will take this paradigm. If a verb begins in a vowel, the connector -*t*- is inserted in the 1st, 2nd, and 3rd persons, singular and plural, *nit-*, *kit-*, and *ot-*, in present tense only. The following is an example of a TI verb conjugation.

wāpantan – *see it* (V-TI)

1S	**ni**wāpantān	I see it
2S	**ki**wāpantān	you see it
3S	**o**wāpantān	she/he sees it
3'S	**o**wāpantāni	his/her ____ sees it
1P	**ni**wāpantā**min**	we (ex) see it
21	**ki**wāpantā**min**	we (in) see it
2P	**ki**wāpantā**m**	you all see it
3P	**o**wāpantā**nāwā**	they see it
3'P	**o**wāpantā**ni**	his/her ____s see it

In the example above, *wāpanta-* is the verb stem. You will notice that the final short vowel -*a* in some TI verbs stems will become a long vowel -*ā* when put in the indicative mode only.

Here are some example sentences using TI verbs in the indicative:

Ninōntān iškotē-otāpan.	*I hear a train.*
Omīcin wāwan.	*She/he is eating an egg.*
Kikihkēntān na?	*Do you know it?*
Owāpantānāwā wāhkāhikan.	*They see a house.*
Nipītōmin nimasinahikan.	*We are bringing my book.*

TENSE AND ASPECT

Tense and aspect pre-verbs can also be used with the indicative and negative indicative modes. The standard verb structure for TI verbs follows this pattern:

Personal prefix	Tense/aspect pre-verbs	Pre-verbs	Verb root/stem	Personal suffix
ni(t)-	kī- (past)			
ki(t)-	ka- (future definite, 1st, 2nd pers)			
o(t)-	ta- (future definite, 3rd pers)			
	wī- (aspect)			

V-TI Indicative Past Tense

wāpantan – *see it*

1S	*ni*kī-wāpantā*n*	*I saw it*
2S	*ki*kī-wāpantā*n*	*you saw it*
3S	*o*kī-wāpantā*n*	*she/he saw it*
3'S	*o*kī-wāpantā*ni*	*his/her _____ saw it*
1P	*ni*kī-wāpantā*min*	*we (ex) saw it*
21	*ki*kī-wāpantā*min*	*we (in) saw it*
2P	*ki*kī-wāpantā*m*	*you all saw it*
3P	*o*kī-wāpantā*nāwā*	*they saw it*
3'P	*o*kī-wāpantā*ni*	*his/her _____s saw it*

Here are some example sentences using TI verbs in the indicative past tense:

Nikī-mīcin napōp.	*I ate soup.*
Kikī-wāpantān na nimahkisin?	*Did you see my shoe?*
Okī-pītōn nimasinahikan.	*She/he brought my book.*
Nikī-pāhkinān wāhsēnikan.	*I opened the window.*

V-TI Indicative Future Definite Tense

nōntan – *(you) hear it*

1S	*ni*ka-nōntā*n*	*I will hear it*
2S	*ki*ka-nōntā*n*	*you will hear it*
3S	*o*ta-nōntā*n*	*she/he will hear it*
3'S	*o*ta-nōntā*ni*	*his/her _____ will hear it*
1P	*ni*ka-nōntā*min*	*we (ex) will hear it*
21	*ki*ka-nōntā*min*	*we (in) will hear it*
2P	*ki*ka-nōntā*m*	*you all will hear it*
3P	*o*ta-nōntā*nāwā*	*they will hear it*
3'P	*o*ta-nōntā*ni*	*his/her _____s will hear it*

V-TI Indicative Aspect

mīcin *– (you) eat it*

1S	*ni***wī**-mīci*n*	*I am going to eat it*
2S	*ki***wī**-mīci*n*	*you are going to eat it*
3S	*o***wī**-mīci*n*	*she/he is going to eat it*
3'S	*o***wī**-mīci*ni*	*his/her _____ is going to eat it*
1P	*ni***wī**-mīci*min*	*we (ex) are going to eat it*
21	*ki***wī**-mīci*min*	*we (in) are going to eat it*
2P	*ki***wī**-mīci*m*	*you all are going to eat it*
3P	*o***wī**-mīci*nāwā*	*they are going to eat it*
3'P	*o***wī**-mīci*ni*	*his/her _____s are going to eat it*

Negative Indicative Mode

In the negative indicative mode, the verb is negated by using the negative particle *kāwin* "no/ not" before the verb and attaching a negative suffix to the end of the verb root/stem. The negative suffix for TI verb roots/stems with the final vowels *-i* and *-o* is *-hsī*. For TI verb root/ stems with the final vowel *-a*, the negative suffix is *-nsī*. *Kāwin* is usually shortened to *kān*.

No.	Particle	Personal prefix	Verb (vowel)	Negative suffix	Personal suffix	Translation
1s	kāwīn	ni-	-i, -o/-a	-hsī/-nsī	-n	*I do not...it*
2s	kāwīn	ki-	-i, -o/-a	-hsī/-nsī	-n	*you do not...it*
3s	kāwīn	o-	-i, -o/-a	-hsī/-nsī	-n	*she/he does not...it*
3's	kāwīn	o-	-i, -o/-a	-hsī/-nsī	-ni	*his/her _____ does not...it*
1P	kāwīn	ni-	-i, -o/-a	-hsī/-nsī	-min	*we (ex) do not...it*
21	kāwīn	ki-	-i, -o/-a	-hsī/-nsī	-min	*we (in) do not...it*
2P	kāwīn	ki-	-i, -o/-a	-hsī/-nsī	-m	*you all do not...it*
3P	kāwīn	o-	-i, -o/-a	-hsī/-nsī	-nāwā	*they do not...it*
3'P	kāwīn	o-	-i, -o/-a	-hsī/-nsī	-ni	*his/her _____s do not...it*

Note: The hyphen is to indicate that the elements are attached to one another.

V-TI with final vowel -i or -o

mīcin – *eat it*

1S	**kāwīn** nimīci**hsī**n	*I do not eat it*
2S	**kāwīn** kimīci**hsī**n	*you do not eat it*
3S	**kāwīn** omīci**hsī**n	*she/he does not eat it*
3's	**kāwīn** omīci**hsī**ni	*his/her _____ does not eat it*
1P	**kāwīn** nimīci**hsī**min	*we* (ex) *do not eat it*
21	**kāwīn** kimīci**hsī**min	*we* (in) *do not eat it*
2P	**kāwīn** kimīci**hsī**m	*you all do not eat it*
3P	**kāwīn** omīci**hsī**nāwā	*they do not eat it*
3'P	**kāwīn** omīci**hsī**ni	*his/her _____s do not eat it*

This pattern is used for TI verbs that contain the final vowel -*i* and -*o* in the verb stem/root (in the example above, *mīci-* is the verb stem). The connector -*t*- rule applies also for verbs that begin in a vowel, only in the present tense.

When a verb with a final vowel -*a* is put in the negative indicative mode, the final -*a* does not become a long vowel as it did in the indicative mode but stays short, as shown in the following example.

V-TI with final vowel -a

wāpantan – *see it*

1S	**kāwīn** niwāpanta**nsī**n	*I do not see it*
2S	**kāwīn** kiwāpanta**nsī**n	*you do not see it*
3S	**kāwīn** owāpanta**nsī**n	*she/he does not see it*
3's	**kāwīn** owāpanta**nsī**ni	*his/her _____ does not see it*
1P	**kāwīn** niwāpanta**nsī**min	*we* (ex) *do not see it*
21	**kāwīn** kiwāpanta**nsī**min	*we* (in) *do not see it*
2P	**kāwīn** kiwāpanta**nsī**m	*you all do not see it*
3P	**kāwīn** owāpanta**nsī**nāwā	*they do not see it*
3'P	**kāwīn** owāpanta**nsī**ni	*his/her _____s do not see it*

When using tense or aspect, the position of the pre-verb is similar to all verb modes.

Negative particle	Personal prefix	Tense/aspect pre-verbs	Pre-verbs	Verb root/ stem	Negative suffix	Personal suffix
kāwīn	ni(t)-	kī-		-i	-hsī	
kān	ki(t)-	ka-		-o	-nsī	
	o(t)-	ta-		-a		
		wī-				

Kāwīn niwāpantansīn omā.	*I don't see it here.*
Kāwīn okī-mīcihsīn napōp.	*She/he did not eat soup.*
Kāwīn okihkēntansīnāwā.	*They do not know it.*
Kāwīn nikī-nōntansīmin otāpān.	*We did not hear a car.*

For extra practise, see the Chapter 16 Exercises on pages 173–174.

CHAPTER

· · · · · · · · · · ·

17

Objectives

- Transitive inanimate verbs (V-TI), continued
- Subjunctive mode
- Negative subjunctive mode

Dialogues

1. Wēkonēn kā-mihkank?
   Okī-mihkān tēhsiwīhakwān.

   What did she/he find?
   She/he found a hat.

2. Ānīhšwīn wēnci-kī-kipahaman iškwāntēm?
   Kihsinā ānīhš.

   Why did you close the door?
   Because it's cold.

3. Ānīhšwīn wēnci-kī-kipahansiwan wāhsēnikan?
   Kī-kišāhtē ānīhš.

   Why didn't you close the window?
   Because it was hot.

Vocabulary

Nāškan.	*(You) fetch it.*	Nātin.	*(You) get it.*
Mihkan.	*(You) find it.*	Ošihtōn.	*(You) make it.*
Āpahcitōn.	*(You) use it.*	Kipahan.	*(You) close it.*

Transitive Inanimate Verbs (V-TI), continued

Chapter 16 introduced transitive inanimate verbs, or V-TI. In this chapter, we will look at the subjunctive and negative subjunctive modes of this verb type, exploring a variety of paradigms to compare present tense, past tense, future definite tense, and aspect.

Subjunctive Mode

Subjunctive mode, as we have seen previously, is used to indicate subordination and is considered less "factual" than the indicative mode. It is used to ask *supplementary questions,* which must be supplemented with an answer. The subjunctive mode is also used in *subordinate clauses,* which are ungrammatical when they stand alone. The subjunctive mode persons are indicated by personal suffixes that are very different from the indicative mode personal affixes.

The personal suffixes for 1st and 2nd persons, singular and plural, differ depending on the final vowel in the verb stem, as shown in the next two tables.

V-TI Subjunctive Mode Paradigm for stems with the final vowel *-i*		
1s	(kīšpin) **-yān**	*(if) I...it*
2s	(kīšpin) **-yan**	*(if) you...it*
3s	(kīšpin) **-t**	*(if) she/he...it*
3's	(kīšpin) **-nit**	*(if) his/her _____...it*
1P	(kīšpin) **-yānk**	*(if) we (ex)...it*
21	(kīšpin) **-yank**	*(if) we (in)...it*
2P	(kīšpin) **-yēk**	*(if) you all...it*
3P	(kīšpin) **-wāt**	*(if) they...it*
3'P	(kīšpin) **-nit**	*(if) his/her _____s...it*

The verb stem for *mīcin* "eat it" is *mīci-*.

mīcin – *eat it*

(kīšpin) mīci**yān**	*(if) I eat it*
(kīšpin) mīci**yan**	*(if) you eat it*
(kīšpin) mīci**t**	*(if) she/he eats it*
(kīšpin) mīci**nit**	*(if) his/her ____ eats it*
(kīšpin) mīci**yānk**	*(if) we (ex) eat it*
(kīšpin) mīci**yank**	*(if) we (in) eat it*
(kīšpin) mīci**yēk**	*(if) you all eat it*
(kīšpin) mīci**wāt**	*(if) they eat it*
(kīšpin) mīci**nit**	*(if) his/her ____s eat it*

V-TI Subjunctive Mode Paradigm for stems with the final vowel -ō		
1s	(kīšpin) -**wãn**	*(if) I...it*
2s	(kīšpin) -**wan**	*(if) you...it*
3s	(kīšpin) -**t**	*(if) she/he...it*
3's	(kīšpin) -**nit**	*(if) his/her _____...it*
1P	(kīšpin) -**wãnk**	*(if) we (ex)...it*
21	(kīšpin) -**wank**	*(if) we (in)...it*
2P	(kīšpin) -**wēk**	*(if) you all...it*
3P	(kīšpin) -**wãt**	*(if) they...it*
3'P	(kīšpin) -**nit**	*(if) his/her _____s...it*

The verbs stem of *pītōn* "bring it" is *pītō-*.

pītōn – *bring it*

(kīšpin) pītō**wãn**	*(if) I bring it*
(kīšpin) pītō**wan**	*(if) you bring it*
(kīšpin) pītō**t**	*(if) she/he brings it*
(kīšpin) pītō**nit**	*(if) his/her _____ brings it*
(kīšpin) pītō**wãnk**	*(if) we (ex) bring it*
(kīšpin) pītō**wank**	*(if) we (in) bring it*
(kīšpin) pītō**wēk**	*(if) you all bring it*
(kīšpin) pītō**wãt**	*(if) they bring it*
(kīšpin) pītō**nit**	*(if) his/her _____s bring it*

V-TI stems/roots with the final vowel -*a* take slightly different person suffixes, as shown below.

V-TI Subjunctive Mode Paradigm for stems with the final vowel -a		
1s	(kīšpin) -**mãn**	*(if) I...it*
2s	(kīšpin) -**man**	*(if) you...it*
3s	(kīšpin) -**nk**	*(if) she/he...it*
3's	(kīšpin) -**minit**	*(if) his/her _____...it*
1P	(kīšpin) -**mãnk**	*(if) we (ex) ...it*
21	(kīšpin) -**mank**	*(if) we (in) ...it*
2P	(kīšpin) -**mēk**	*(if) you all...it*
3P	(kīšpin) -**mowãt**	*(if) they...it*
3'P	(kīšpin) -**minit**	*(if) his/her _____s...it*

The verb stem for *wāpantan* "see it" is *wāpanta-*.

wāpantan – *see it*

(kīšpin) wāpanta**mān**	*(if) I see it*
(kīšpin) wāpanta**man**	*(if) you see it*
(kīšpin) wāpanta**nk**	*(if) she/he sees it*
(kīšpin) wāpanta**minit**	*(if) his/her _____ sees it*
(kīšpin) wāpanta**mānk**	*(if) we (ex) see it*
(kīšpin) wāpanta**mank**	*(if) we (in) see it*
(kīšpin) wāpanta**mēk**	*(if) you all see it*
(kīšpin) wāpanta**mowāt**	*(if) they see it*
(kīšpin) wāpanta**minit**	*(if) his/her _____s see it*

Here are some example sentences in the subjunctive mode:

Wēkonēn nōntaman?	*What do you hear?*
Āwēnēn mīcit?	*Who is eating it?*
Nika-cīhkēntam **kīšpin pītōwan nimasinahikan**.	*I will be happy **if you bring my book**.*
Kīšpin mihkamān nimahkisin, nika-kīwē.	***If I find my shoe**, I will go home.*

The first two examples are supplementary questions, and in the last two examples the subordinate clauses are in bold.

TENSE AND ASPECT

Tense and aspect pre-verbs can also be attached to the front of the verbs in the subjunctive mode. The vowel in tense/aspect pre-verbs goes through an initial change when used in the subjunctive mode, as seen here:

present	no pre-verb
past	kā-
future definite (will)	kē-
aspect (going to)	wā-

The following charts are examples of V-TI in the subjunctive mode and in the tenses and aspect.

V-TI Subjunctive Past Tense

nāškan – *(you) fetch it*

1S	(kīšpin) **kā**-nāška*mān*	*(if) I fetched it...*
2S	(kīšpin) **kā**-nāška*man*	*(if) you fetched it...*
3S	(kīšpin) **kā**-nāška*nk*	*(if) she/he fetched it...*
3'S	(kīšpin) **kā**-nāška*minit*	*(if) his/her _____ fetched it...*
1P	(kīšpin) **kā**-nāška*mānk*	*(if) we (ex) fetched it...*
21	(kīšpin) **kā**-nāška*mank*	*(if) we (in) fetched it...*
2P	(kīšpin) **kā**-nāška*mēk*	*(if) you all fetched it...*
3P	(kīšpin) **kā**-nāška*mowāt*	*(if) they fetched it...*
3'P	(kīšpin) **kā**-nāška*minit*	*(if) his/her _____s fetched it...*

V-TI Subjunctive Future Definite Tense

nātin – *(you) get it*

1S	(kīšpin) **kē**-nāti*yān*	*(if) I will get it...*
2S	(kīšpin) **kē**-nāti*yan*	*(if) you will get it...*
3S	(kīšpin) **kē**-nāti*t*	*(if) she/he will get it...*
3'S	(kīšpin) **kē**-nāti*nit*	*(if) his/her _____ will get it...*
1P	(kīšpin) **kē**-nāti*yānk*	*(if) we (ex) will get it...*
21	(kīšpin) **kē**-nāti*yank*	*(if) we (in) will get it...*
2P	(kīšpin) **kē**-nāti*yēk*	*(if) you all will get it...*
3P	(kīšpin) **kē**-nāti*wāt*	*(if) they will get it...*
3'P	(kīšpin) **kē**-nāti*nit*	*(if) his/her _____s will get it ...*

V-TI Subjunctive Aspect

ošihtōn – *(you) make it*

1S	(kīšpin) **wā**-ošihtō*wān*	*(if) I am going to make it...*
2S	(kīšpin) **wā**-ošihtō*wan*	*(if) you are going to make it...*
3S	(kīšpin) **wā**-ošihtō*t*	*(if) she/he is going to make it...*
3'S	(kīšpin) **wā**-ošihtō*nit*	*(if) his/her _____ is going to make it...*
1P	(kīšpin) **wā**-ošihtō*wānk*	*(if) we (ex) are going to make it...*
21	(kīšpin) **wā**-ošihtō*wank*	*(if) we (in) are going to make it...*
2P	(kīšpin) **wā**-ošihtō*wēk*	*(if) you all are going to make it...*
3P	(kīšpin) **wā**-ošihtō*wāt*	*(if) they are going to make it...*
3'P	(kīšpin) **wā**-ošihtō*nit*	*(if) his/her _____s are going to make it...*

Wēkonēn kā-nōntaman?	*What did you hear?*
Ānahpī kē-wāpantamānk?	*When will we see it? (ex)*
Nikā-kipahan iškwāntēm.	*I will close the door.*
Kīšpin nāskamān, kika-āpahcitōn na?	*If I fetch it, will you use it?*

Negative Subjunctive Mode

Negative subjunctive mode is the opposite of the subjunctive mode. It is used to negate a subordinate clause. The particle *kāwīn* is *not* used with this mode. The negative suffix *-hsi* is attached before the personal suffix to verb stems ending in *i* and *ō*, and the negative suffix *-nsi* is attached to verb stems ending in *a*. As with the subjunctive, the persons are shown using the suffixes. The personal suffixes for the negative subjunctive mode differ from those in the subjunctive mode, as shown in the following table. Interrogative pronouns and conjunctional particles are also used with this mode.

V-TI Negative Subjunctive Mode Paradigm		
1s	(kīšpin) **-hsi**wān	*(if) I do not...it*
2s	(kīšpin) **-hsi**wan	*(if) you do not...it*
3s	(kīšpin) **-hsi**k	*(if) she/he does not...it*
3's	(kīšpin) **-hsi**nik	*(if) his/her _____ does not...it*
1P	(kīšpin) **-hsi**wānk	*(if) we (ex) do not...it*
21	(kīšpin) **-hsi**wank	*(if) we (in) do not...it*
2P	(kīšpin) **-hsi**wēk	*(if) you all do not...it*
3P	(kīšpin) **-hsi**wāt	*(if) they do not...it*
3'P	(kīšpin) **-hsi**nik	*(if) his/her _____s do not...it*

V-TI Negative Subjunctive Present Tense

wāpantan – *(you) see it*

1s	(kīšpin) wāpanta**nsi**wān	*(if) I do not see it*
2s	(kīšpin) wāpanta**nsi**wan	*(if) you do not see it*
3s	(kīšpin) wāpanta**nsi**k	*(if) she/he does not see it*
3's	(kīšpin) wāpanta**nsi**nik	*(if) his/her _____ does not see it*
1P	(kīšpin) wāpanta**nsi**wānk	*(if) we (ex) do not see it*
21	(kīšpin) wāpanta**nsi**wank	*(if) we (in) do not see it*
2P	(kīšpin) wāpanta**nsi**wēk	*(if) you all do not see it*
3P	(kīšpin) wāpanta**nsi**wāt	*(if) they do not see it*
3'P	(kīšpin) wāpanta**nsi**nik	*(if) his/her _____s do not see it*

Tense and aspect pre-verbs are also used with the subjunctive mode, and they are placed before the verb.

present	no pre-verb
past	kā-
future definite (will)	kē-
aspect (going to)	wā-

The following charts are examples of V-TI in the negative subjunctive mode and in the tenses and aspect.

Negative Subjunctive Past Tense

pītōn – *(you) bring it*

1S	(kīšpin) **kā**-pītō**hsi**wān	*(if) I did not bring it...*
2S	(kīšpin) **kā**-pītō**hsi**wan	*(if) you did not bring it...*
3S	(kīšpin) **kā**-pītō**hsi**k	*(if) she/he did not bring it...*
3's	(kīšpin) **kā**-pītō**hsi**nik	*(if) his/her _____ did not bring it...*
1P	(kīšpin) **kā**-pītō**hsi**wānk	*(if) we (ex) did not bring it...*
21	(kīšpin) **kā**-pītō**hsi**wank	*(if) we (in) did not bring it...*
2P	(kīšpin) **kā**-pītō**hsi**wēk	*(if) you all did not bring it...*
3P	(kīšpin) **kā**-pītō**hsi**wāt	*(if) they did not bring it...*
3'P	(kīšpin) **kā**-pītō**hsi**nik	*(if) his/her _____s did not bring it...*

Negative Subjunctive Future Definite Tense

mīcin – *(you) eat it*

1S	(kīšpin) kē-mīci**hsi**wān	*(if) I will not eat it...*
2S	(kīšpin) kē-mīci**hsi**wan	*(if) you will not eat it...*
3S	(kīšpin) kē-mīci**hsi**k	*(if) she/he will not eat it...*
3's	(kīšpin) kē-mīci**hsi**nik	*(if) his/her _____ will not eat it...*
1P	(kīšpin) kē-mīci**hsi**wānk	*(if) we (ex) will not eat it...*
21	(kīšpin) kē-mīci**hsi**wank	*(if) we (in) will not eat it...*
2P	(kīšpin) kē-mīci**hsi**wēk	*(if) you all will not eat it...*
3P	(kīšpin) kē-mīci**hsi**wāt	*(if) they will not eat it...*
3'P	(kīšpin) kē-mīci**hsi**nik	*(if) his/her _____s will not eat it...*

Negative Subjunctive Aspect

mihkan – *(you) find it*

1S	(kīšpin) **wā**-mihka**nsi**wān	*(if) I am not going to find it...*
2S	(kīšpin) **wā**-mihka**nsi**wan	*(if) you are not going to find it...*
3S	(kīšpin) **wā**-mihka**nsi**k	*(if) she/he is not going to find it...*
3's	(kīšpin) **wā**-mihka**nsi**nik	*(if) his/her _____ is not going to find it...*
1P	(kīšpin) **wā**-mihka**nsi**wānk	*(if) we (ex) are not going to find it...*
21	(kīšpin) **wā**-mihka**nsi**wank	*(if) we (in) are not going to find it...*
2P	(kīšpin) **wā**-mihka**nsi**wēk	*(if) you all are not going to find it...*
3P	(kīšpin) **wā**-mihka**nsi**wāt	*(if) they are not going to find it...*
3'P	(kīšpin) **wā**-mihka**nsi**nik	*(if) his/her _____s are not going to find it...*

This form can also be negated without using a negative suffix by using the pre-verb ēkā- instead and adding the personal suffixes from the subjunctive mode, as in the following table.

Negative Subjunctive Using ēkā- and the Subjunctive Personal Suffixes

wāpantan – *(you) see it*

1s	(kīspin) **ēkā**-wāpamak	*(if) I do not see him/her/it...*
2s	(kīspin) **ēkā**-wāpamat	*(if) you do not see him/her/it...*
3s	(kīspin) **ēkā**-wāpamāt	*(if) she/he does not see him/her/it...*
3's	(kīspin) **ēkā**-wāpamānit	*(if) his/her _____ does not see him/her/it...*
1P	(kīspin) **ēkā**-wāpamankit	*(if) we (ex) do not see him/her/it...*
21	(kīspin) **ēkā**-wāpamankit	*(if) we (in) do not see him/her/it...*
2P	(kīspin) **ēkā**-wāpamāyēk	*(if) you all do not see him/her/it...*
3P	(kīspin) **ēkā**-wāpamāwāt	*(if) they do not see him/her/it...*
3'P	(kīspin) **ēkā**-wāpamānit	*(if) his/her _____s do not see him/her/it...*

Kīspin wāpamāhsiwāk nōnkom,
   nika-wāpamā wāpank.
(or using ēkā-)
Kīspin ēkā-wāpamak nōnkom, nika-wāpamā wāpank.

If I don't see him/her today,
   I will see him/her tomorrow.

Kīspin pāhpihāhsiwat, kān kita-niškātišihsī.

If you don't laugh at him,
   he will not be angry/mad.

For extra practise, see the Chapter 17 Exercises on page 175.

EXERCISES

Chapter 1 Exercises

1. Write a word in Saulteaux containing each vowel and translate:

   a: _____

   ā: _____

   i: _____

   ī: _____

   o: _____

   ō: _____

   ē: _____

2. Write a word in Saulteaux containing the consonant and translate.

   c: _____

   hc: _____

   k: _____

   hk: _____

p: _____

hp: _____

t: _____

ht: _____

s: _____

hs: _____

š: _____

hš: _____

h: _____

m: _____

n: _____

w: _____

y: _____

Chapter 2 Exercises

1. List six (6) minimal pairs and two (2) near-minimal sets in Saulteaux and translate.

   Minimal pairs:

   _____   _____

   _____   _____

   _____   _____

   _____   _____

   _____   _____

   _____   _____

   Near-minimal sets:

   _____   _____

   _____   _____

2. Write the dialogue in Saulteaux:

   How are you now? _____

   Nothing is wrong, you then? _____

   I'm fine. _____

   Thanks. _____

   I'm grateful to you. _____

   I'll see you again. _____

   Okay, I'll see you again. _____

Chapter 3 Exercises

1. Answer the following in English.

Nānan šikwa nīwin, ānīn minik?

_____

Nīmitana ahsi nīš šikwa nihso, ānīn minik?

_____

Nikotwāhso otāhpinan nānan, ānīn minik?

_____

Nikotwāhk otāhpinan nīmitana ahsi pēšik, ānīn minik?

_____

Nīmitana ahsi nīš šikwa mitāhso ahsi šānkahso, ānīn minik?

_____

2. Answer the following in Saulteaux.

Nānwāpik otāhpin nīwāpik, ānīn minik?

_____

Nīwin pīwāpihkōns otāhpin nīš pīwāpihkōns, ānīn minik?

_____

Nikotwāhswāpik otāhpin nānwāpik, ānīn minik?

_____

Nihsomitana-tahswāpik otāhpin nīštana-tahswāpik, ānīn minik?

_____

Mitāhso pīwāpihkōns otāhpin nānan pīwāpihkōns, ānīn minik?

_____

Chapter 4 Exercises

1. Write the following nouns in Saulteaux in the singular and plural forms.

	Singular	*Plural*
dog	_____	_____
cat	_____	_____
woman	_____	_____
man	_____	_____
shoe	_____	_____
jacket	_____	_____
pants	_____	_____
shirt	_____	_____
sock	_____	_____
cup	_____	_____
plate	_____	_____
tablespoon	_____	_____
knife	_____	_____
fork	_____	_____
horse	_____	_____
house	_____	_____
car	_____	_____
table	_____	_____
chair	_____	_____
bed	_____	_____

2. Write the following phrases in Saulteaux.

dogs and cats: _____

plates/bowls and cups: _____

sock and shoe: _____

man and woman: _____

house and car: _____

Chapter 5 Exercises

1. Write the English sentences in Saulteaux and translate the Saulteaux sentences to English.

This is a big house.

_____

Who are those ones?

_____

That is a big pig in the distance.

_____

What is this?

_____

That is a chair in the distance.

_____

What are those in the distance?

_____

Awēnēn awē?

_____

Wēkonēnan iniwēti?

_____

Wāpikwānīn iniwē.

_____

Onkowē mitāhsak.

_____

Owē wāhkāhikan.

_____

Awē šīhšīp.

_____

2. List the seven (7) personal pronouns and translate:

1S _____   1P _____

2S _____   21 _____

                                   2P _____

3S _____   3P _____

Chapter 6 Exercises

1. Write the nouns in the **S**ingular, **P**lural, **D**iminutive and **L**ocative forms.

star

S: _____

P: _____

D: _____

L: _____

book

S: _____

P: _____

D: _____

L: _____

pants

S: _____

P: _____

D: _____

L: _____

flower

S: _____

P: _____

D: _____

L: _____

2. Write the English sentences in Saulteaux and translate the Saulteaux sentences to English.

The darn puppy is in the house.

_____

That cup is on the little table.

_____

The books are in the cupboard.

_____

That boat is in the water.

_____

Iškotē-otāpan mīhkanānk.

_____

Ihkwē atāwēwikamikōnk.

_____

Oškinīkīns awē otāpānink.

_____

Maci-ihkwē kīšikōnk.

_____

Chapter 7 Exercises

1. Put the family terms in the possessive forms. The first one is done for you.

1s   nitānihs   my daughter

2s   _____   _____

3s   _____   _____

3's   _____   _____

1P   _____   _____

21   _____   _____

2P   _____   _____

3P   _____   _____

3'P   _____   _____

1s   nōhkō   my grandmother

2s   _____   _____

3s   _____   _____

3's   _____   _____

1P   _____   _____

21   _____   _____

2P   _____   _____

3P   _____   _____

3'P   _____   _____

2. Translate the following sentences to English.

Awēnēn kōhkō?

_____

Awēnēn kimihšōmihš?

_____

Nikosihs awē.

_____

Kimihšōmē awē.

_____

Mi-awē nimāmāyēnsinān.

_____

Chapter 8 Exercises

1. Write the English sentences in Saulteaux and translate the Saulteaux sentences to English.

Come play (pl)!

_____

Let's sing and (let's) dance!

_____

Don't look at him (pl)!

_____

The children played outside.

_____

Did your older sister eat?

_____

It's not warm today.

_____

Kāwīn niwī-išāhsīmin atāwēwikamikōnk nōnkom, mākišā wāpank.

_____

Kīšpin āpawāhk wāpank, ihkwēsēnsak ta-anohkīwak akocīnk.

_____

Išātā āhkosīwikamikōnk, ninōntē-mawatihšwā nimāmāyēns.

_____

Kīšpin anōhkīhsiwank nōnkom, kēko išātā minihkwēwikamikōnk.

_____

Owāpantān wāhkāhikan iwēti.

_____

Atōhpowināhkōnk ahtēwan kimasinahikanan.

_____

Chapter 9 Exercises

1. Write the particles in Saulteaux.

today	_____	tomorrow	_____
yesterday	_____	tonight	_____
last night	_____	morning	_____
and/now	_____	again	_____
right now	_____	right away	_____
yes	_____	no	_____
correct/right	_____	not correct	_____
before	_____	after	_____
the same	_____	different	_____
please	_____	thanks	_____

2. Translate the following sentences to English.

Kihci-pawātan!

_____

Ani-kīwēn šikwa!

_____

Kēko kihci-kīwanimohkēn!

_____

Niwī-anta-atāwēmin wāpank.

_____

Mākišā wāpank ta-kihci-anohkī.

_____

Chapter 10 Exercises

1. Write the English sentences in Saulteaux and translate the Saulteaux sentences to English.

It's a cloudy day today.

_____

It will snow tomorrow.

_____

It was not cold yesterday.

_____

It was not Wednesday, it was Tuesday.

_____

It's going to be 8:00 soon.

_____

It will drizzle this morning.

_____

Ta-awan na wāpank?

_____

Kāwīn kimiwansinōn tipihkahk.

_____

Nīpawa ta-sōkihpon nōnkom.

_____

Kikišēp kī-sōkihpon, kī-āpawā tahs .

_____

Chapter 11 Exercises

1. Write the English sentences in Saulteaux and translate the Saulteaux sentences to English.

    When will it blow snow?

    _____

    Where did it storm?

    _____

    It's not going to rain today, maybe tomorrow it will rain.

    _____

    If it's cold tomorrow, I will stay home.

    _____

    When is it going to be a nice day?

    _____

    Ānahpī wā-kimiwank?

    _____

    Nikī-apimin kā-kihci-nōtink.

    _____

    Kīšpin kihci-sōkihpohk, kān nika-kīwēhsī.

    _____

    Kīšpin sōkihpohk, ta-āpawā.

    _____

    Ānīhšwīn kā-nōtink?

    _____

Chapter 12 Exercises

1. Put the verb listed in the imperative and negative imperative modes.

minihkwē – *she/he is drinking*

Imperative and Negative Imperative Modes		
	Saulteaux	**English**
I.S.		
I.P.		
I.I.		
N.I.S.		
N.I.P.		
N.I.I.		

2. Conjugate the following verbs in the modes and tenses listed.

pāhpi – *she/he is laughing*

Indicative Mode—Present Tense		
	Saulteaux	**English**
1s		
2s		
3's		
1P		
21		
2P		
3P		
3'P		

antotam – *she/he is listening*

	Negative Indicative Mode—Past Tense	
	Saulteaux	**English**
1s		
2s		
3's		
1P		
21		
2P		
3P		
3'P		

Chapter 13 Exercises

1. Conjugate the following verbs in the modes and tenses listed.

wīhsini – *she/he is eating*

Subjunctive Mode—Aspect		
	Saulteaux	**English**
1s		
2s		
3's		
1P		
21		
2P		
3P		
3'P		

cīhkēntam – *she/he is happy*

Negative Subjunctive Mode—Past Tense		
	Saulteaux	**English**
1s		
2s		
3's		
1P		
21		
2P		
3P		
3'P		

2. Write the following questions in Saulteaux.

Who was sleeping?

_____

Where is my brother going to work?

_____

Why did you run?

_____

Chapter 14 Exercises

1. Put the verb listed in the imperative and negative imperative modes.

   wīcih – *help him/her/it*

Imperative and Negative Imperative Modes		
	Saulteaux	**English**
I.S.		
I.P.		
I.I.		
N.I.S.		
N.I.P.		
N.I.I.		

2. Conjugate the following verbs in the modes and tenses listed.

   mihkaw – *find him/her/it*

Indicative Mode—Future Definite Tense		
	Saulteaux	**English**
1s		
2s		
3's		
1P		
21		
2P		
3P		
3'P		

antotaw – *listen to him/her/it*

Negative Indicative Mode—Past Tense	
Saulteaux	**English**
1s	
2s	
3's	
1P	
21	
2P	
3P	
3'P	

Chapter 15 Exercises

1. Conjugate the following verbs in the modes and tenses listed.

pīh – *wait for him/her/it*

Subjunctive Mode—Present Tense		
	Saulteaux	English
1s		
2s		
3's		
1P		
21		
2P		
3P		
3'P		

antotaw – *listen to him/her/it*

Negative Subjunctive Mode—Past Tense		
	Saulteaux	English
1s		
2s		
3's		
1P		
21		
2P		
3P		
3'P		

Chapter 16 Exercises

1. Put the verbs listed in the imperative and negative imperative modes.

   kanawāpantan – *look at it*

Imperative and Negative Imperative Modes		
	Saulteaux	**English**
I.S.		
I.P.		
I.I.		
N.I.S.		
N.I.P.		
N.I.I.		

2. Conjugate the following verbs in the modes and tenses listed.

   kihkēntan – *know it*

Indicative Mode—Aspect		
	Saulteaux	**English**
1s		
2s		
3's		
1P		
21		
2P		
3P		
3'P		

pītōn – *bring it*

	Saulteaux	English
Negative Indicative Mode—Past Tense		
1s		
2s		
3's		
1P		
21		
2P		
3P		
3'P		

Chapter 17 Exercises

1. Conjugate the following verbs in the modes and tenses listed.

nōntan – *hear it*

Subjunctive Mode—Future Definite Tense		
	Saulteaux	**English**
1s		
2s		
3's		
1P		
21		
2P		
3P		
3'P		

mīcin – *eat it*

Negative Subjunctive Mode—Future Definite Tense		
	Saulteaux	**English**
1s		
2s		
3's		
1P		
21		
2P		
3P		
3'P		

VERB CONJUGATION PATTERNS
(V-AI, V-TA, AND V-TI)

Animate Intransitive Verbs (V-AI)

IMPERATIVE AND NEGATIVE IMPERATIVE MODE (COMMANDS AND NEGATIVE COMMANDS)

AI verbs are listed in the 3rd person singular (3s), the **bare verb.**

Verbs ending in any vowel (*a, ā, i, ī, o, ō, ē*)			
I.S.		-n	*you* (sg)...
I.P.		-k	*you all* (pl)...
I.I.		-tā	*let's...*
N.I.S.	kēko	-hkēn	*(you) don't...*
N.I.P.	kēko	-hkēk	*(you all) don't...*
N.I.I.	kēko	-tā	*let's not...*

Verbs ending in *-am*			
I.S.		-n*	*you* (sg)...
I.P.		-mok	*you all* (pl)...
I.I.		-ntā*	*let's...*
N.I.S.	kēko	-nkēn*	*(you) don't...*
N.I.P.	kēko	-nkēk*	*(you all) don't...*
N.I.I.	kēko	-ntā*	*let's not...*

* m in verb is dropped

Verbs ending in -hšin

I.S.		-in	*you (sg)...*
I.P.		-ik	*you all (pl)...*
I.I.		-ntā	*let's...*
N.I.S.	kēko	-ihkēn	*(you) don't...*
N.I.P.	kēko	-ihkēk	*(you all) don't...*
N.I.I.	kēko	-itā	*let's not...*

INDICATIVE MODE (STATEMENTS AND YES/NO QUESTIONS)

For verbs beginning in **vowels**, the connector -*t*- is **added** in present tense **only**.

Verbs ending in any vowel (*a, ā, i, ī, o, ō, ē*)

1s	ni(t)-*		*I am...*
2s	ki(t)-*		*you are...*
3s	(bare verb)		*she/he is...*
3's		-wan	*his/her (NA sg) is...*
1P	ni(t)-	-min	*we (ex) are...*
21	ki(t)-	-min	*we (in) are...*
2P	ki(t)-	-m	*you all (pl) are...*
3P		-wak	*they are...*
3'P		-wah	*his/her (NA pl) are...*

* verbs ending in short *i* and *o*, the vowel drops in 1s and 2s

Verbs ending in -am

1s	ni(t)-		*I am...*
2s	ki(t)-		*you are...*
3s	(bare verb)		*she/he is...*
3's		-mōn	*his/her (NA sg) is...*
1P	ni(t)-	-in	*we (ex) are...*
21	ki(t)-	-in	*we (in) are...*
2P	ki(t)-	-(ā)m*	*you all (pl) are...*
3P		-mōk	*they are...*
3'P		-mōh	*his/her (NA pl) are...*

* the short *a* in the verb root changes to a long *ā* in 2P

Verbs ending in -*hšin*			
1s	ni(t)-		*I am...*
2s	ki(t)-		*you are...*
3s	(bare verb)		*she/he is...*
3's		-ōn	*his/her* (NA sg) *is...*
1P	ni(t)-	-imin	*we* (ex) *are...*
21	ki(t)-	-imin	*we* (in) *are...*
2P	ki(t)-	-im	*you all* (pl) *are...*
3P		-ōk	*they are...*
3'P		-ōh	*his/her* (NA pl) *are...*

NEGATIVE INDICATIVE MODE (NEGATIVE STATEMENTS)

Verbs ending in any vowel (*a, ā, i, ī, o, ō, ē*) (the negative suffix is -*hsī*)			
1s	kāwīn ni(t)-*	-hsī	*I am not...*
2s	kāwīn ki(t)-*	-hsī	*you are not...*
3s	kāwīn (bare verb)	-hsī	*she/he is not...*
3's	kāwīn	-hsīwan	*his/her* (NA sg) *is not...*
1P	kāwīn ni(t)-	-hsīmin	*we* (ex) *are not...*
21	kāwīn ki(t)-	-hsīmin	*we* (in) *are not...*
2P	kāwīn ki(t)-	-hsīm	*you all* (pl) *are not...*
3P	kāwīn	-hsīwak	*they are not...*
3'P	kāwīn	-hsīwah	*his/her* (NA pl) *are not...*

* verbs ending in short *i* and *o*, the vowel drops in 1s and 2s

Verbs ending in -*am* (the *m* is dropped; the negative suffix is –*nsī*)

1s	kāwīn ni(t)-	-nsī	*I am not...*
2s	kāwīn ki(t)-	-nsī	*you are not...*
3s	kāwīn (bare verb)	-nsī	*she/he is not...*
3's	kāwīn	-nsīwan	*his/her* (NA sg) *is not...*
1P	kāwīn ni(t)-	-nsīmin	*we* (ex) *are not...*
21	kāwīn ki(t)-	-nsīmin	*we* (in) *are not...*
2P	kāwīn ki(t)-	-nsīm	*you all* (pl) *are not...*
3P	kāwīn	-nsīwak	*they are not...*
3'P	kāwīn	-nsīwah	*his/her* (NA pl) *are not...*

Verbs ending in -*hšin* (the negative suffix is -*sī*)

1s	kāwīn ni(t)-	-sī	*I am not...*
2s	kāwīn ki(t)-	-sī	*you are not...*
3s	kāwīn (bare verb)	-sī	*she/he is not...*
3's	kāwīn	-sīwan	*his/her* (NA sg) *is not...*
1P	kāwīn ni(t)-	-sīmin	*we* (ex) *are not...*
21	kāwīn ki(t)-	-sīmin	*we* (in) *are not...*
2P	kāwīn ki(t)-	-sīm	*you all* (pl) *are not...*
3P	kāwīn	-sīwak	*they are not...*
3'P	kāwīn	-sīwah	*his/her* (NA pl) *are not...*

SUBJUNCTIVE MODE (SUPPLEMENTARY QUESTIONS AND SUBORDINATE CLAUSES)

Some verbs that begin in a vowel will take an initial change. The change occurs in the first syllable of the verb and only in the **present tense**.

Verbs ending in the vowels *a, ā, i, ī, ē*

1s	(kīšpin)	-yān	*(if) I...*
2s	(kīšpin)	-yan	*(if) you...*
3s	(kīšpin)	-t	*(if) she/he...*
3's	(kīšpin)	-nit	*(if) his/her (NA sg)...*
1P	(kīšpin)	-yānk	*(if) we (ex)...*
21	(kīšpin)	-yank	*(if) we (in)...*
2P	(kīšpin)	-yēk	*(if) you all (pl)...*
3P	(kīšpin)	-wāt	*(if) they...*
3'P	(kīšpin)	-nit	*(if) his/her (NA pl)...*

Verbs ending in the vowels *o* and *ō*

1s	(kīšpin)	-wān	*(if) I...*
2s	(kīšpin)	-wan	*(if) you...*
3s	(kīšpin)	-t	*(if) she/he...*
3's	(kīšpin)	-nit	*(if) his/her (NA sg)...*
1P	(kīšpin)	-wānk	*(if) we (ex)...*
21	(kīšpin)	-wank	*(if) we (in)...*
2P	(kīšpin)	-wēk	*(if) you all (pl)...*
3P	(kīšpin)	-wāt	*(if) they...*
3'P	(kīšpin)	-nit	*(if) his/her (NA pl)...*

Verbs ending in *-am*

1s	(kīšpin)	-ān	*(if) I...*
2s	(kīšpin)	-an	*(if) you...*
3s	(kīšpin)	-nk	*(if) she/he...*
3's	(kīšpin)	-init	*(if) his/her (NA sg)...*
1P	(kīšpin)	-ānk	*(if) we (ex)...*
21	(kīšpin)	-ank	*(if) we (in)...*
2P	(kīšpin)	-wēk	*(if) you all (pl)...*
3P	(kīšpin)	-owāt	*(if) they...*
3'P	(kīšpin)	-init	*(if) his/her (NA pl)...*

Verbs ending in *-hšin*			
1s	(kīšpin)	-ān	*(if) I...*
2s	(kīšpin)	-an	*(if) you...*
3s	(kīšpin)	-k	*(if) she/he...*
3's	(kīšpin)	-init	*(if) his/her* (NA sg)...
1P	(kīšpin)	-ānk	*(if) we* (ex)...
21	(kīšpin)	-ank	*(if) we* (in)...
2P	(kīšpin)	-ēk	*(if) you all* (pl)...
3P	(kīšpin)	-iwāt	*(if) they...*
3'P	(kīšpin)	-init	*(if) his/her* (NA pl)...

NEGATIVE SUBJUNCTIVE MODE (NEGATIVE SUBORDINATE CLAUSES)

Verbs ending in any vowel (*a, ā, i, ī, o, ō, ē*) (the negative suffix is *-hsi*)			
1s	(kīšpin)	-hsiwān	*(if) I do not...*
2s	(kīšpin)	-hsiwan	*(if) you do not...*
3s	(kīšpin)	-hsik	*(if) she/he does not...*
3's	(kīšpin)	-hsinik	*(if) his/her* (NA sg) *does not...*
1P	(kīšpin)	-hsiwānk	*(if) we* (ex) *do not...*
21	(kīšpin)	-hsiwank	*(if) we* (in) *do not...*
2P	(kıśpin)	-hsiwēk	*(if) you all* (pl) *do not...*
3P	(kīšpin)	-hsikwā	*(if) they do not...*
3'P	(kīšpin)	-hsinik	*(if) his/her* (NA pl) *do not...*

Verbs ending in *-am* (the *m* is dropped; the negative suffix is *–nsi*)			
1s	(kīšpin)	-nsiwān	*(if) I do not...*
2s	(kīšpin)	-nsiwan	*(if) you do not...*
3s	(kīšpin)	-nsik	*(if) she/he does not...*
3's	(kīšpin)	-nsinik	*(if) his/her* (NA sg) *does not...*
1P	(kīšpin)	-nsiwānk	*(if) we* (ex) *do not...*
21	(kīšpin)	-nsiwank	*(if) we* (in) *do not...*
2P	(kīšpin)	-nsiwēk	*(if) you all* (pl) *do not...*
3P	(kīšpin)	-nsikwā	*(if) they do not...*
3'P	(kīšpin)	-nsinik	*(if) his/her* (NA pl) *do not...*

Verbs ending in *-hšin* (the negative suffix is *-si*)			
1s	(kīšpin)	-siwãn	*(if) I do not…*
2s	(kīšpin)	-siwan	*(if) you do not…*
3s	(kīšpin)	-sik	*(if) she/he does not…*
3's	(kīšpin)	-sinik	*(if) his/her (NA sg) does not…*
1P	(kīšpin)	-siwãnk	*(if) we (ex) do not…*
21	(kīšpin)	-siwank	*(if) we (in) do not…*
2P	(kīšpin)	-siwēk	*(if) you all (pl) do not…*
3P	(kīšpin)	-sikwã	*(if) they do not…*
3'P	(kīšpin)	-sinik	*(if) his/her (NA pl) do not…*

Another way to conjugate AI verbs in the negative subjunctive mode is to use the **basic subjunctive mode patterns** and the pre-verb *ēkā-*; a negative suffix is *not* needed when *ēkā-* is used.

Negative subjunctive with the pre-verb *ēkā-*			
1s	ēkā-	-yãn/-wãn/-ãn	*I do not…*
2s	ēkā-	-yan/-wan/-an	*you do not…*
3s	ēkā-	-t/-nk	*she/he does not…*
3's	ēkā-	-nit/-init	*his/her (NA sg) does not…*
1P	ēkā-	-yãnk/-wãnk/-ãn	*we (ex) do not…*
21	ēkā-	-yank/-wank/-an	*we (in) do not…*
2P	ēkā-	-yēk/-wēk/-m/-n	*you all (pl) do not…*
3P	ēkā-	-wāt/-owāt/-iwāt	*they do not…*
3'P	ēkā-	-nit/-init	*his/her (NA pl) do not…*

Transitive Animate Verbs (V-TA)

IMPERATIVE AND NEGATIVE IMPERATIVE MODE

Verb stems ending in consonants -*m, -w, -n, -h* in the imperative singular			
I.S.		-m/-w/-n/-h	*(you)...him/her/it*
I.P.		-ik	*(you all)...him/her/it*
I.I.		-ātā	*let's...him/her/it*
N.I.S.	kēko	-āhkēn	*(you) don't ...him/her/it*
N.I.P.	kēko	-āhkēk	*(you all) don't...him/her/it*
N.I.I.	kēko	-ātā	*let's not...him/her/it*

Verb stems ending in the consonants -*s* and -*š* in the imperative singular (the -*s/-š* is dropped and -*n* is added for I.P. to N.I.I.)			
I.S.		-s/-š	*(you)...him/her/it*
I.P.		(-s/-š → n)ik	*(you all)...him/her/it*
I.I.		(-s/-š → n)ātā	*let's...him/her/it*
N.I.S.	kēko	(-s/-š → n)āhkēn	*(you) don't ...him/her/it*
N.I.P.	kēko	(-s/-š → n)āhkēk	*(you all) don't...him/her/it*
N.I.I.	kēko	(-s/-š → n)ātā	*let's not...him/her/it*

Verb stems ending in the vowel -*o* in the imperative singular (the -*o* is dropped and -*wā* is added for I.P. to N.I.I.)			
I.S.		-o	*(you)...him/her/it*
I.P.		(-o → wā)hk	*(you all)...him/her/it*
I.I.		(-o → wā)tā	*let's...him/her/it*
N.I.S.	kēko	(-o → wā)hkēn	*(you) don't ...him/her/it*
N.I.P.	kēko	(-o → wā)hkēk	*(you all) don't...him/her/it*
N.I.I.	kēko	(-o → wā)tā	*let's not...him/her/it*

Verb stems ending in consonants –m, –w, –n, –h in the imperative singular

1s	ni(t)-	-ā	*I...him/her/it*
2s	ki(t)-	-ā	*you...him/her/it*
3s	o(t)-	-ān	*she/he...him/her/it*
3's	o(t)-	-āni	*his/her (NA sg)...him/her/it*
1P	ni(t)-	-ānān	*we (ex)...him/her/it*
21	ki(t)-	-ānān	*we (in)...him/her/it*
2P	ki(t)-	-āwā	*you all (pl)...him/her/it*
3P	o(t)-	-āwān	*they...him/her/it*
3'P	o(t)-	-āni	*his/her (NA pl)...him/her/it*

Verb stems ending in consonants –s or –š in the imperative singular
(the final -s/-š → -n when put into the indicative mood)

1s	ni(t)-	-nā	*I...him/her/it*
2s	ki(t)-	-nā	*you...him/her/it*
3s	o(t)-	-nān	*she/he...him/her/it*
3's	o(t)-	-nāni	*his/her (NA sg)...him/her/it*
1P	ni(t)-	-nānān	*we (ex)...him/her/it*
21	ki(t)-	-nānān	*we (in)...him/her/it*
2P	ki(t)-	-nāwā	*you all (pl)...him/her/it*
3P	o(t)-	-nāwān	*they...him/her/it*
3'P	o(t)-	-nāni	*his/her (NA pl)...him/her/it*

Verb stems ending in the vowel –o in the imperative singular
(the final -o → -wā when put into the indicative mood)

1s	ni(t)-	-wā	*I...him/her/it*
2s	ki(t)-	-wā	*you...him/her/it*
3s	o(t)-	-wān	*she/he...him/her/it*
3's	o(t)-	-wāni	*his/her (NA sg)...him/her/it*
1P	ni(t)-	-wānān	*we (ex)...him/her/it*
21	ki(t)-	-wānān	*we (in)...him/her/it*
2P	ki(t)-	-wāwā	*you all (pl)...him/her/it*
3P	o(t)-	-wāwān	*they...him/her/it*
3'P	o(t)-	-wāni	*his/her (NA pl)...him/her/it*

NEGATIVE INDICATIVE MODE (NEGATIVE STATEMENTS)

Basic paradigm for TA verbs in the negative indicative, but follow the rules for the different verbs stems (the negative suffix is *-hsī* in 1s, 2s, and 3s and *–hsi* in 3's to 3'ᴘ)			
1s	kāwīn ni(t)-	-(ā)hsī	*I do not...him/her/it*
2s	kāwīn ki(t)-	-(ā)hsī	*you do not...him/her/it*
3s	kāwīn o(t)-	-(ā)hsīn	*she/he does not...him/her/it*
3's	kāwīn o(t)-	-(ā)hsini	*his/her (NA sg) does not...him/her/it*
1P	kāwīn ni(t)-	-(ā)hsiwānān	*we (ex) do not...him/her/it*
21	kāwīn ki(t)-	-(ā)hsiwānān	*we (in) do not...him/her/it*
2P	kāwīn ki(t)-	-(ā)hsiwāwā	*you all (pl) do not...him/her/it*
3P	kāwīn o(t)-	-(ā)hsiwāwān	*they do not...him/her/it*
3'P	kāwīn o(t)-	-(ā)hsini	*his/her (NA pl) do not...him/her/it*

SUBJUNCTIVE MODE (SUPPLEMENTARY QUESTIONS AND SUBORDINATE CLAUSES)

Basic paradigm for TA verbs in the subjunctive, but follow the rules for the different verbs stems			
1s	(kīšpin)	-(a)k*	*(if) I...him/her/it*
2s	(kīšpin)	-(a)t*	*(if) you...him/her/it*
3s	(kīšpin)	-(ā)t	*(if) she/he...him/her/it*
3's	(kīšpin)	-(a)nıt	*(if) his/her (NA sg)...him/her/it*
1P	(kīšpin)	-(a)nkit*	*(if) we (ex)...him/her/it*
21	(kīšpin)	-(a)nkit*	*(if) we (in)...him/her/it*
2P	(kīšpin)	-(ā)yēk	*(if) you all (pl)...him/her/it*
3P	(kīšpin)	-(ā)wāt	*(if) they...him/her/it*
3'P	(kīšpin)	-(ā)nit	*(if) his/her (NA pl)...him/her/it*

*In the 1st and 2nd persons, the direction marker changes from a long *-ā* to a short *-a*.

NEGATIVE SUBJUNCTIVE MODE (NEGATIVE SUBORDINATE CLAUSES)

Basic paradigm for TA verbs in the negative subjunctive, but follow the rules for the different verbs stems (the negative suffix is *-hsi*)			
1s	(kīšpin)	-(ā)hsiwak	*(if) I do not...him/her/it*
2s	(kīšpin)	-(ā)hsiwat	*(if) you do not...him/her/it*
3s	(kīšpin)	-(ā)hsihk	*(if) she/he does not...him/her/it*
3's	(kīšpin)	-(ā)hsinik	*(if) his/her (NA sg) does not...him/her/it*
1P	(kīšpin)	-(ā)hsinit	*(if) we (ex) do not...him/her/it*
21	(kīšpin)	-(ā)hsinit	*(if) we (in) do not...him/her/it*
2P	(kīšpin)	-(ā)hsiwāyēk	*(if) you all (pl) do not...him/her/i*
3P	(kīšpin)	-(ā)hsiyēkwā	*(if) they do not...him/her/it*
3'P	(kīšpin)	-(ā)hsinik	*(if) his/her (NA pl) do not...him/her/it*

This can also be negated with the pre-verb *ēkā-*. When using *ēkā-*, the negative suffix is *not needed* and the subjunctive mode person suffixes are applied.

Transitive Inanimate Verbs (V-TI)

IMPERATIVE AND NEGATIVE IMPERATIVE MODE (COMMANDS AND NEGATIVE COMMANDS)

TI verbs are listed in the imperative singular (I.S.).

Verb stems ending in vowels *-i* and *-ō*			
I.S.		-n	*(you)...it*
I.P.		-k	*(you all)...it*
I.I.		-tā	*let's...it*
N.I.S.	kēko	-hkēn	*(you) don't ...it*
N.I.P.	kēko	-hkēk	*(you all) don't...it*
N.I.I.	kēko	-tā	*let's not...it*

Verb stems ending in vowel -*a*			
I.S.		-n	*(you)...it*
I.P.		-mok	*(you all)...it*
I.I.		-ntā	*let's...it*
N.I.S.	kēko	-nkēn	*(you) don't ...it*
N.I.P.	kēko	-nkēk	*(you all) don't...it*
N.I.I.	kēko	-ntā	*let's not...it*

INDICATIVE MODE (STATEMENTS AND YES/NO QUESTIONS)

For TI verb stems that end in -*a*, the -*a* → -*ā* when put in the indicative mode only. For verbs beginning in vowels, the connector -*t*- is added in present tense only.

All TI Verb stems			
1s	ni(t)-	-n	*I...it*
2s	ki(t)-	-n	*you...it*
3s	o(t)-	-n	*she/he...it*
3's	o(t)-	-ni	*his/her* (NA sg)*...it*
1P	ni(t)-	-min	*we* (ex)*...it*
21	ki(t)-	-min	*we* (in)*...it*
2P	ki(t)-	-m	*you all* (pl)*...it*
3P	o(t)-	-nāwā	*they...it*
3'P	o(t)-	-ni	*his/her* (NA pl)*...it*

NEGATIVE INDICATIVE MODE (NEGATIVE STATEMENTS)

Verb stems ending in -*i* and -*ō* (the negative suffix is -*hsī*)			
1s	kāwīn ni(t)-	-hsīn	*I do not...it*
2s	kāwīn ki(t)-	-hsīn	*you do not...it*
3s	kāwīn o(t)-	-hsīn	*she/he does not...it*
3's	kāwīn o(t)-	-hsīni	*his/her* (NA sg) *does not...it*
1P	kāwīn ni(t)-	-hsīmin	*we* (ex) *do not...it*
21	kāwīn ki(t)-	-hsīmin	*we* (in) *do not...it*
2P	kāwīn ki(t)-	-hsīm	*you all* (pl) *do not...it*
3P	kāwīn o(t)-	-hsīnāwā	*they do not...it*
3'P	kāwīn o(t)-	-hsīni	*his/her* (NA pl) *do not...it*

Verb stems ending in -*a* (the negative suffix is -*nsī*)

1s	kāwīn ni(t)-	-nsīn	*I do not...it*
2s	kāwīn ki(t)-	-nsīn	*you do not...it*
3s	kāwīn o(t)-	-nsīn	*she/he does not...it*
3′s	kāwīn o(t)-	-nsīni	*his/her (NA sg) does not...it*
1P	kāwīn ni(t)-	-nsīmin	*we (ex) do not...it*
21	kāwīn ki(t)-	-nsīmin	*we (in) do not...it*
2P	kāwīn ki(t)-	-nsīm	*you all (pl) do not...it*
3P	kāwīn o(t)-	-nsīnāwā	*they do not...it*
3′P	kāwīn o(t)-	-nsīni	*his/her (NA pl) do not...it*

SUBJUNCTIVE MODE (SUPPLEMENTARY QUESTIONS AND SUBORDINATE CLAUSES)

Verb stems ending in the vowel -*i*

1s	(kīšpin)	-yān	*(if) I...it*
2s	(kīšpin)	-yan	*(if) you...it*
3s	(kīšpin)	-t	*(if) she/he...it*
3′s	(kīšpin)	-nit	*(if) his/her (NA sg)...it*
1P	(kīšpin)	-yānk	*(if) we (ex)...it*
21	(kīšpin)	-yank	*(if) we (in)...it*
2P	(kīšpin)	-yēk	*(if) you all (pl)...it*
3P	(kīšpin)	-wāt	*(if) they...it*
3′P	(kīšpin)	-nit	*(if) his/her (NA pl)...it*

Verb stems ending in the vowel -*ō*

1s	(kīšpin)	-wān	*(if) I...it*
2s	(kīšpin)	-wan	*(if) you...it*
3s	(kīšpin)	-t	*(if) she/he...it*
3′s	(kīšpin)	-nit	*(if) his/her (NA sg)...it*
1P	(kīšpin)	-wānk	*(if) we (ex)...it*
21	(kīšpin)	-wank	*(if) we (in)...it*
2P	(kīšpin)	-wēk	*(if) you all (pl)...it*
3P	(kīšpin)	-wāt	*(if) they...it*
3′P	(kīšpin)	-nit	*(if) his/her (NA pl)...it*

Verb stems ending in the vowel -a			
1s	(kīšpin)	-mān	*(if) I...it*
2s	(kīšpin)	-man	*(if) you...it*
3s	(kīšpin)	-nk	*(if) she/he...it*
3's	(kīšpin)	-minit	*(if) his/her (NA sg)...it*
1P	(kīšpin)	-mānk	*(if) we (ex)...it*
21	(kīšpin)	-mank	*(if) we (in)...it*
2P	(kīšpin)	-mēk	*(if) you all (pl)...it*
3P	(kīšpin)	-mowāt	*(if) they...it*
3'P	(kīšpin)	-minit	*(if) his/her (NA pl)...it*

NEGATIVE SUBJUNCTIVE MODE (NEGATIVE SUBORDINATE CLAUSES)

Verb stems ending in -i and -ō (the negative suffix is -hsi)			
1s	(kīšpin)	-hsiwān	*(if) I do not...it*
2s	(kīšpin)	-hsiwan	*(if) you do not...it*
3s	(kīšpin)	-hsik	*(if) she/he does not...it*
3's	(kīšpin)	-hsinik	*(if) his/her (NA sg) does not...it*
1P	(kīšpin)	-hsiwānk	*(if) we (ex) do not...it*
21	(kīšpin)	-hsiwank	*(if) we (in) do not...it*
2P	(kīšpin)	-hsiwēk	*(if) you all (pl) do not...it*
3P	(kīšpin)	-hsiwāt	*(if) they do not...it*
3'P	(kīšpin)	-hsinik	*(if) his/her (NA pl) do not...it*

Verb stems ending in -a (the negative suffix is -nsi)			
1s	(kīšpin)	-nsiwān	*(if) I do not...it*
2s	(kīšpin)	-nsiwan	*(if) you do not...it*
3s	(kīšpin)	-nsik	*(if) she/he does not...it*
3's	(kīšpin)	-nsinik	*(if) his/her (NA sg) does not...it*
1P	(kīšpin)	-nsiwānk	*(if) we (ex) do not...it*
21	(kīšpin)	-nsiwank	*(if) we (in) do not...it*
2P	(kīšpin)	-nsiwēk	*(if) you all (pl) do not...it*
3P	(kīšpin)	-nsiwāt	*(if) they do not...it*
3'P	(kīšpin)	-nsinik	*(if) his/her (NA pl) do not...it*

This can also be negated with *ēkā-* and the subjunctive suffixes; a negative suffix is not needed when using the pre-verb *ēkā-*.

VOCABULARY LIST

The following abbreviations are for the grammatical items here:

ex – exclusive	pl – plural	s.t. – something
in – inclusive	PN – pronoun	V-AI – animate intransitive verb
NA – animate noun	PV – pre-verb	V-II – inanimate intransitive verb
NI – inanimate noun	sg – singular	V-TA – transitive animate verb
PC – particle	s.o. – someone	V-TI – transitive inanimate verb

A

ahām: okay (PC)

ahkawē: first/beforehand (PC)

ahkihk: a pail/kettle (NA)

ahkiwēnsī: old man (NA)

ahpī: when (PC)

ahsam: feed him/her/it (V-TA)

ahsamā: she/he is being fed (V-AI)

ahsēmā: tobacco (NA)

ahsēmāns: cigarette (NA)

ahsi: used between numbers for higher digits (PC)

ahsin: a rock (NA)

ahtē: it is sitting (V-II)

akihk: nasal mucus/snot (NA)

akim: count him/her/it (V-TA)

akincikīhswān: a calendar (NI)

akintāhso: she/he is counting (V-AI)

akintāhsowin: number (NI)

akocīnk: outside (PC)

akōcikan: a cupboard (NI)

amihk: a beaver (NA)

amo: eat it (V-TA)

ampē: come (PC)

anamihā: she/he is praying (V-AI)

anamihcikē: she/he is reading (V-AI)

anamihē-kīšikat: it is Sunday (V-II)

anāmihī: underneath (PC)

anank: a star (NA)

anankōnskā: it is starry (V-II)

ani-: away from, directional (PV)

anihšināpē: First Nation person (NA)

anihšināpēmo: she/he speaks Saulteaux (T-AI)

anihšināpēmowin: Saulteaux language (NI)

anihšināpēwi-kīšikat: First Nations Day; it is First Nations Day (V-II)

animohš: a dog (NA)

anohkī: she/he is working (V-AI)

anōhkī: she/he asks s.o. to work for him/her (V-AI)

anōhš: ask him/her/it (V-TA)

anta-: go and... (PV)

antonēh: (you) look for him/her/it (V-TA)

antotam: she/he is listening (V-AI)

antotaw: (you) listen to him/her/it (V-TA)
api: she/he is sitting (V-AI)
apinōcī: a child (NA)
apinōcīwi-kīšikat: Child's Day; it is Child's Day (V-II)
ašēkīwē: she/he goes back (V-AI)
atāwē: she/he is buying (V-AI)
atāwēwikamik: a store (NI)
atōhpowināhk: a table (NI)
awahš: go away (PC)
awahšēwē: she/he goes out of sight (V-AI)
awahšimē: get worse (PC)
awahš-nāko: the day before yesterday (PC)
awahš-wāpank: the day after tomorrow (PC)
awan: it is foggy (V-II)
awanipīhsā: it is drizzling (V-II)
awē: this/that (one) (PN)
awēnēn: who (PN)
awēti: that (one) in the distance (PN)
awiya: someone (PC)
awīh: lend him/her (V-TA)
ayapi: she/he is at home (V-AI)
ayā: she/he is (there) (V-AI)
ayān: have it (V-TI)
ayāw: (you) have him/her/it (V-TI)
ayēhkosi: she/he is tired from work (V-AI)

Ā

āhkosi: she/he is sick (V-AI)
āhkosīwikamik: hospital (NA)
āhpihci: really/very (PC)
ākim: snowshoe (NA)
āmō: a bee (NA)
ānahpī: when (PN)
ānīhš: why (PC)
ānīhšwīn: why (PN)
ānint: some (PC)
ānīn: how/what (PN)
āntēk: a crow (NA)
ānti: where (PN)
āpahcih: (you) use him/her/it (V-TA)
āpahcitōn: use it (V-TI)
āpawā: it is warm (V-II)

āpihta: half (PC)
āpihta-nīpinowi-kīsihs: July; Mid-Summer Moon
āpihta-pipōniwi-kīsihs: January; Mid-Winter Moon
āpihtawohsē: it is Wednesday (V-II)
āpihtā-tipihkat: it is midnight (V-II)
āpitink: once/one more time (PC)
āša: already (PC)
āsokan: a bridge (NI)

C

cāhcāmo: she/he is coughing (V-AI)
cākišan: (you) burn it (V-TI)
cākišo: she/he is burning (V-AI)
cākiš(w): (you) burn him/her/it (V-TA)
cākitē: it's burning (V-II)
ci-: can/able to (PV)
cīhkēntam: she/he is happy (V-AI)
cīhkēntamok wīhtikēyēk: Happy Anniversary; Be happy you're married!
cīhkēntan: (you) be happy about it (V-TI)
cīhkēntan kā-tipiškaman: Happy Birthday; Be happy it is your birthday!
cīhkēntan mīkwēciwi-kīšikahk: Thanksgiving Day; Be happy it is giving thanks day!
cīhkēntan ocīnitiwi-kīšikahk: New Year's Day; Be happy it is kissing day!
cīhkēntan omāmāwi-kīšikahk: Mother's Day; Be happy it is Mother's day!
cīhkēntan opāpāwi-kīšikahk: Father's Day; Be happy it is Father's day!
cīkahī: beside (PC)
cīmān: a canoe/boat (NI)
cīpayikanān: skeleton (NI pl)
cīpayiwi-kīšikat: Halloween; it's ghost day (V-II)
cīpwā-: before (PC/PV)

Ĕ

ēhta: only (PC)
ēmihkwān: tablespoon (NA)
ēnikōns: ant (NA)
ēnikok: try hard (PC)

ēniwēk: just so/so-so (PC)
ēntānit: his/her ___'s (NA) home
ēntāt: his/her home
ēntāwāt: their home
ēntāyan: your home
ēntāyank: our (in) home
ēntāyān: my home
ēntāyānk: our (ex) home
ēntāyēk: your (pl) home

I

ihkwē: a woman (NA)
ihkwēsēns: little girl (NA)
imā: there (PC)
inawēmākan: relative (NA)
inini: a man (NA)
iniwē: those (PN)
iniwēti: those in the distance (PN)
inkiwē: those (ones) (PN)
inkiwēti: those (ones) in the distance (PN)
išā: she/he goes (there) (V-AI)
iši-: to, directional (PC/PV)
išihsē: it turns, expresses time (hours) (V-II)
išinākosi: she/he looks like (V-AI)
išinihkāso: she/he is called (V-AI)
išiwēpahk: reference to weather (V-II)
iškonikan: reserve/left over land (NI)
iškotē: fire (NI)
iškotēw-otāpān: train (NI)
iškwāntēm: a door (NI)
iškwā: after (PC)
iškwā-anamihē-kīšikat: Monday; it is a day after
 Prayer day (V-II)
iškwāc: last (PC)
išpimink: up/above (PC)
iwē: that (thing) (PN)
iwēti: that (thing) in the distance (PN)

Ī

īhay: expression of fear (PC)
ītok: probably (PC)
īwiti: over there (PC)

K

kahkina: all/everyone (PC)
kakwē: to try (PC)
kakwēcim: (you) ask him/her/it (V-TA)
kanātahkīwi-kīšikat: Canada Day; it is pure/
 clean day (V-II)
kanōš: (you) call him/her/it (V-TA)
kawaci: she/he is cold (V-AI)
kawihšimo: she/he is going to bed (V-AI)
kayē: also/too (PC)
kāmahsi: not yet (PC)
kān awiya: no one (PC)
kān kwayak: not correct/not right (PC)
kān pāhpiš: not at all/not even (PC)
kān wīhkā: not ever (PC)
kāwīn (kān): no/not (PC)
kāwē: she/he is jealous (V-AI)
kēhcinā: probably (PC)
kēhtitawēn: suddenly (PC)
kēkā: almost/just about (PC)
kēkēt: really/surely (PC)
kēko: don't (PC)
kēkō: something (PC)
kēmā: or (PC)
kēyāpi: still/yet (PC)
kihci-: big/great/huge (PC)
kihci-kihkēntāsōwikamik: University; great
 knowledge building (NI)
kīhkaci: she/he is cold (V-AI)
kihkēnim: (you) know him/her/it (V-TA)
kihkēntan: (you) know it (V-TI)
kihkēntāhso: she/he has knowledge (V-AI)
kihkinahomākē: she/he is teaching (V-AI)
kihkinahomākēwikamik: school; teaching
 building (NI)
kihsayē: your older brother
kihsayēyinān: our older brother (in)
kihsayēyiwā: your older brother (pl)
kihsinā: it is cold (V-II)
kikišēp: this morning (PC)
kimiwan: it is raining (V-II)
kimōti: she/he is stealing (V-AI)
kiniw: eagle (NA)

kinōsē: jackfish (NA)

kipahan: (you) close it (V-TI)

kipitin: (you) stop him/her/it (V-TA)

kišāhtē: it is hot (outdoors) (V-II)

kišihtē: it is hot (indoors) (V-II)

kišīpīkahikan: soap (NI pl)

kišišihkē: she/he makes it hot with fire (V-AI)

kišišihtē: she/he has hot feet (V-AI)

kišišo: she/he is hot or fevered (V-AI)

kitānihs: your daughter (sg)

kitānihsinān: our daughter (in)

kitānihsiwā: your daughter (pl)

kīhsohkān: clock (NA)

kīhsohkānēns: watch (NA)

kīhtwām: again (PC)

kīkito: she/he is speaking (V-AI)

kīkō: fish (NA)

kīmōhc: on the sly (PC)

kīn: you (PN)

kīnawā: you (PN pl)

kīnawint: us (PN in)

kīsihs: sun (NA)

kīšihtē: it is cooking (V-II)

kīšikat: it is day (V-II)

kīšikāhtē: it is moonlight (V-II)

kīšpin: if (PC)

kīwē: she/he is going home (V-AI)

kīwētin: north direction

kīwētinonk: in the north

konakē: wondering (PC)

kotink: at one time (PC)

kotinō: something (PC)

kotwā: probably (PC)

kotwāmihkwat: it is storming (V-II)

kōhkōhš: pig (NA)

kwayak: correct/right (PC)

M

maci-: bad/evil (PV)

mahīnkan: wolf (NA)

mahkatēwā: it is black (V-II)

mahkatēwāhsim: black horse (NA)

mahkatēwisi: she/he/it is black (V-AI)

mahkisin: a shoe (NI)

mahkwa: bear (NA)

makohšēwi-kīsihs: December; Feasting Moon

makohšēwi-kīšīkat: Christmas Day; it is feasting day (V-II)

manisikēwi-kīsihs: August; Hay-cutting Moon

manitōwi-kīsihs: December; Spirit/God Moon

manitōwi-kīšikat: Christmas Day; it is Spirit/God day (V-II)

manki-: big/huge (PV)

mankitōn: big mouth (NA)

mankitōnē: she/he has a big mouth (V-AI)

mantāmin: corn (NA)

masinahikan: book (NI)

maškihki: medicine (NI)

maškihkīwinini: doctor (NA)

maškīkō: swamp (NI)

mawatihšiwē: she/he is visiting (V-AI)

mawi: she/he is crying (V-AI)

mayaki-: strange (PV)

mācā: she/he is leaving (V-AI)

mācī-: to start (PV)

mākišā: maybe (PC)

māmawopi: she/he sits together/is meeting (V-AI)

māmāhšīhš: any old way/carelessly (PC)

māmow: together (PC)

mātinawē-kīšikat: Saturday; it is ration day (V-II)

mēkwā: right now (PC)

mēkwāškaw: (you) meet him/her/it (V-TA)

mēwinša: long ago (PC)

mi-: it is so/so (PC/PV)

mihkan: (you) find it (V-TI)

mihkaw: (you) find him/her/it (V-TA)

mihtik: tree (NA); stick (NI)

mihtikōn: sticks (NA)

mikisiwi-kīsihs: February; Condor/Eagle Moon

minah: (you) give him/her/it a drink (V-TA)

minihkwācikan: cup (NI)

minihkwē: she/he is drinking (V-AI)

minik: to do with quantity (PC)

mino-: good/well/nice (PV)

mino-kīšikat: it is a nice day (V-II)

mino-manitōwi-kīšikat: Merry Christmas; it is good Spirit/God day (V-II)

minšiwē: all over (PC)

mintimowē: old lady (NA)

mišihsē: turkey (NA)

miskosi: she/he/it is red (V-AI)

miskwā: it is red (V-II)

miskwi: blood (NI)

mištatim: horse (NA)

mitāhs: pants (NA)

mitāhso: ten, 10

mitāhso ahsi pēšik-išihsē: it is eleven o'clock (V-II)

mitāhso ahsi nīš-išihsē: it is twelve o'clock (V-II)

mitāhso-išihsē: it is ten o'clock (V-II)

mitāhso pīwāpihkōns: ten cents, 10¢

mitāhswāhk: one thousand, 1000

mitāhswāhk-tahswāpik: one thousand dollars, $1000

mitāhswāpik: ten dollars, $10

mīcin: (you) eat it (V-TI)

mīhkana: road (NI)

mīkwēc: thanks (PC)

mīkwēciwi-kīšikat: Thanksgiving Day; it is giving thanks day (V-II)

mīnankē: yes (PC)

mīnawā: again (PC)

mīš: (you) give it to him/her/it (V-TA)

mōhkahan: it is sunrise (V-II)

mōhkomān: knife (NI)

mōns: moose (NA)

mōnsōk kā-wīcīntiwāt-kīsihs: September; Moose-mating Moon

mwētahš: after (PC)

N

na: question marker (PC)

nakamo: she/he/it is singing (V-AI)

nakiškaw: (you) meet him/her/it (V-TA)

nanāhitōn: (you) fix it (V-TI)

nanāhkotam: she/he is grateful/thankful (V-AI)

nanāntok: all kinds (PC)

napōp: soup (NI)

nawac: more/kind of (PC)

nāha: right, question marker (PC)

nānamitana: fifty, 50

nānamitana-tahswāpik: fifty dollars, $50

nānan: five, 5

nānan-išihsē: it is five o'clock (V-II)

nānan pīwāpihkōns: five cents, 5¢

nānāhtē: Northern Lights

nāno-kīšikat: it is Friday (V-II)

nānwāhk: five hundred, 500

nānwāhk-tahswāpik: five hundred dollars, $500

nānwāpik: five dollars, $5

nāškan: (you) fetch it (V-TI)

nāškaw: (you) fetch him/her/it (V-TA)

nātin: (you) get it (V-TI)

nāwahī: in the center/middle (PC)

nāwihkwē: it is noon (V-II)

nēyāp: return/as before (PC)

nicān: my nose (NI)

nicīštatēyāp: my muscle (NI)

nihkan: my bone (NI)

nihkāhkikan: my chest (NI)

nihkāt: my leg (NI)

nihki-kīsihs: March; Goose Moon

nihkokwan: my shin (NI)

nihkon: my liver (NI)

nihkwēkan: my neck (NI)

nihpan: my lung (NI)

nihpihkwan: my back (NI)

nihsankwan: my cheek (NI)

nihsayē: my older brother

nihsayēyinān: our older brother (ex)

nihsā: (you) kill him/her/it (V-TA)

nihsimihs: my daughter-in-law

nihso: three, 3

nihso-išihsē: it is three o'clock (V-II)

nihso-kīšikat: Wednesday; it is the third day (V-II)

nihsomitana: thirty, 30

nihsomitana-tahswāpik: thirty dollars, $30

nihso pīwāpihkōns: three cents, 3¢

nihso šōniyāns: seventy-five cents, 75¢; three little monies

nihswāhk: three hundred, 300

nihswāhk-tahswāpik: three hundred dollars, $300
nihswāhso: eight, 8
nihswāhso-išihsē: it is eight o'clock (V-II)
nihswāhsomitana: eighty, 80
nihswāhsomitana-tahswāpik: eighty dollars, $80
nihswāhso pīwāpihkōns: eight cents, 8¢
nihswāhswāhk: eight hundred, 800
nihswāhswāpik: eight dollars, $8
nihswāpik: three dollars, $3
nihšinē: always/all the time (PC)
nihšitotam: she/he understands (V-AI)
nihtihšīns: my navel (NI)
nikanakīnk: my face (NI)
nikā: my mother
nikihtik: my knee (NI)
nikosihs: my son
nikotwāhk: one hundred, 100
nikotwāhk-tahswāpik: one hundred dollars, $100
nikotwāhso: six, 6
nikotwāhso-išihsē: it is six o'clock (V-II)
nikotwāhso-kīsikat: Saturday; it is the sixth day (V-II)
nikotwāhsomitana: sixty, 60
nikotwāhsomitana-tahswāpik: sixty dollars, $60
nikotwāhso pīwāpihkōns: six cents, 6¢
nikotwāhswāhk: six hundred, 600
nikotwāhswāpik: six dollars, $6
nikwīmē: my namesake
nimāmā: my mother
nimāmāyēns: my (maternal) aunt, my "little" mother
nimihsat: my stomach (NI)
nimihsē: my older sister
nimihšōmē: my (paternal) uncle
nimihšōmihš: my grandfather
nimisāpiwin: my eyebrow (NI)
nimisāpiwinān: my eyelash (NI)
nimiskwīm: my blood (NI)
ninakākositān: my sole (foot)(NI)
ninakišīn: my intestines (NI)
ninān: my calf (shin) (NI)
ninihk: my arm (NI)
nininc: my hand (NI)
ninincīns: my thumb (NI)

nininkwan: my son-in-law
ninisīkinincān: my finger (NI)
ninisīkisitān: my toe (NI)
ninīcānihš: my child
ninīkīk: my parent
ninkāpīhan: west direction
ninkāpīhanonk: in the west
ninkwakwat: it is cloudy (V-II)
ninkwan: my nephew
ninōhsē: my (maternal) aunt
ninōhsēyēns: my little grandchild
ninōnkan: my hip (NI)
ninōsihs: my grandchild
nipā: she/he is sleeping (V-AI)
nipāpā: my father
nipēpēm: my baby
nipēwin: a bed (NI)
nipi: water (NI)
nipikay: my rib (NI)
nipwām: my thigh (NI)
nisahī: under/lower (PC)
nisit: my foot (NI)
nisīmēns: my younger sibling
nišihsē: my (maternal) uncle or father-in-law
nišikohš: my (paternal) aunt or mother-in-law
nišīkan: my lower back (NI)
niškahtik: my forehead (NI)
niškatay: my skin (NI)
niškāns: my fingernail (NA)
niškātiši: she/he is angry/mad (V-AI)
niškīnsik: my eye (NI)
ništikwān: my head (NI)
nitatikwākan: my spine (NI)
nitawak: my ear (NI)
nitawēmā: my female (cross) cousin
nitāmikan: my chin (NI)
nitānihs: my daughter
nitānihsinān: our daughter (ex)
nitānkōpicikan: my great-grandparent or my great-grandchild
nitānkwē: my female cousin (female speaker) or my sister-in-law
nitēh: my heart (NI)

nitēnaniw: my tongue (NI)

nitinawēmākan: my relative

nitinimākan: my shoulder (NI)

nitintāwā: my in-law

nitiskwēyāp: my vein (NI)

nitīh: my rear (NI)

nitōhkoš: my kidney (NI)

nitōhšim: my nephew

nitōhšimihkwēm: my niece

nitōn: my mouth (NI)

nitōnēns: my lip (NI)

nitōntan: my heel (NI)

nitōsihs: my aunt (uncle's wife)

nitōskwan: my elbow (NI)

nitōtēm: my friend

nitōtōhšim: my breast (NA)

niwīcīwākan: my partner

niwīnin: my fat (NI)

niwīnisihsan: my hair (NI)

niwīnitip: my brain (NI)

niwīpitan: my tooth (NI)

niwīškway: my bladder (NI)

nīcānihš: child (NA)

nīhcī: my brother, brethren (NA)

nīhtā: my male cousin (male speaker) or my brother-in-law

nīhtāwihš: my male (cross) cousin

nīkān: first (PC)

nīkānahī: in front (PC)

nīmi: she/he is dancing (V-AI)

nīmitana: forty, 40

nīmitana-tahswāpik: forty dollars, $40

nīn: me (PN)

nīnawint: us (PN ex)

nīnim: my brother-in-law

nīnimōns: my sweetheart

nīpawa: a lot (PC)

nīpawi: she/he is standing (V-AI)

nīpin: it is summer (V-II)

nīpīns: leaf (NI)

nīš: two, 2

nīš-išihsē: it is two o'clock (V-II)

nīšo-kīšikat: Tuesday; it is the second day (V-II)

nīš pīwāpihkōns: two cents, 2¢

nīš šōniyāns: fifty cents, 50¢; two little monies

nīštana: twenty, 20

nīštana-tahswāpik: twenty dollars, $20

nīšwāhk: two hundred, 200

nīšwāhk-tahswāpik: two hundred dollars, $200

nīšwāhso: seven, 7

nīšwāhso-išihsē: it is seven o'clock (V-II)

nīšwāhsomitana: seventy, 70

nīšwāhsomitana-tahswāpik: seventy dollars, $70

nīšwāhso pīwāpihkōns: seven cents, 7¢

nīšwāhswāhk: seven hundred, 700

nīšwāhswāpik: seven dollars, $7

nīšwāpik: two dollars, $2

nīwāhk: four hundred, 400

nīwāhk-tahswāpik: four hundred dollars, $400

nīwāpik: four dollars, $4

nīwin: four, 4

nīwin-išihsē: it is four o'clock (V-II)

nīwin pīwāpihkōns: four cents, 4¢

nīyaw: my body (NI)

nīyo-kīšikat: Thursday; it is the fourth day (V-II)

nōhkō: my grandmother

nōhs: my father

nōmaya: a little while ago (PC)

nōnkom: today (PC)

nōntan: (you) hear it (V-TI)

nōntaw: (you) hear him/her/it (V-TA)

nōntē-: to want (PV)

nōntēhšin: she/he is tired (V-AI)

nōtin: it is windy (V-II)

o

ocīntiwi-kīšikat: New Year's Day; it is kissing day (V-II)

ohkan: bone (NI)

ohpwākan: pipe (NA)

ohsayēyan: his/her older brother

ohsayēyini: his/her ___'s (NA sg) older brother

ohsayēyiwān: their older brother

ohsayēyiwānīn: his/her ___s' (NA pl) older brother

okicahī: on top (PC)

okihkinahomākē: teacher (NA)

okimā: boss/Treaty Chief (NA)

okimāhkān: chief (NA)

omahkahkī: frog (NA)

omahkahkīwi-kīsihs: April; Frog Moon

omaškīkō: Cree person (NA)

omā: here (PC)

omāmāwi-kīšikat: Mother's Day; it is Mother's Day (V-II)

onāhkohšin: it is evening (V-II)

onākan: dish/bowl (NI)

onci-: from/for (PV)

onkowē: these (ones) (PN)

onowē: these (things) (PN)

onšām: because (PC)

opāpāwi-kīšikat: Father's Day; it is Father's Day (V-II)

opwāman: his/her thighs (NI)

opwāmān: she/he cannot convince him/her (V-TA)

osāwan: south direction

osāwanonk: in the south

osāwaškosi: she/he/it is blue/green (V-AI)

osāwaškwā: it is blue/green (V-II)

osāwā: it is yellow/brown (V-II)

osāwisi: she/he/it is yellow/brown (V-AI)

ošaškwēhtō: apple (NA)

ošipinikāwi-kīsihs: June; Blooming Moon

ošipıhikanāhk: pencil (NA)

ošihtōn: (you) make it (V-TI)

oškinīkīns: little boy (NA)

otamino: she/he is playing (V-AI)

otaminōwikamik: recreation hall (NI)

otayan: his/her dog (pet) (NA)

otāhpin: (you) take it (V-TI)

otāhpinā: (you) take him/her/it (V-TA)

otānānk: behind (PC)

otānihsan: his/her daughter

otānihsiwān: their daughter

otānihsiwāni: his/her ___'s (NA sg) daughter

otānihsiwānīn: his/her ___s' (NA pl) daughter

otāpān: car (NI)

otāpānāhk: a wagon (NA)

otēhimin: strawberry (NI)

owē: this (thing) (PN)

ō

ōcīns: house fly (NA)

ōtēna: town/village (NI)

p

pahkān: different (PC)

pahkitēh: (you) hit him/her/it (V-TA)

pahkwēšikan: bannock (NA)

pakān: peanut/nut (NA)

pankihšimon: it is sunset (V-II)

pankihšimonk: in the west

pankihšin: she/he is falling (V-AI)

pankitō : she/he is quiet (V-AI)

pankī: a little (PC)

papakowān: shirt (NI)

pāhkāhakwān: chicken (NA)

pāhkinan: (you) open it (V-TI)

pāhpi: she/he is laughing (V-AI)

pāhpih: (you) laugh at him/her/it (V-TA)

pānimā: later (PC)

pāškišikan: gun (NI)

pēhkā: wait (PC)

pēhkiš: as well/all the while (PC)

pēhso: nearby (PC)

pēšik: one, 1

pēšik-išihsē: it is one o'clock (V-II)

pēšiko: alone (PC)

pēšiko-kīšikat: Monday; it is the first day (V-II)

pēšik pīwāpihkōns: one cent, 1¢

pēšik šōniyāns: twenty-five cents, 25¢; one little money

pēšikwan: the same (PC)

pēšikwāpik: one dollar, $1

pi-: toward, directional (PC)

pihcīnāko: yesterday (PC)

pimicahī: alongside (PC)

pimipahtō: she/he/it is running (V-AI)

pimohsē: she/he/it is walking (V-AI)

pinākwēwi-kīsihs: October; Combing Moon

pinēhsī: bird (NA)

pinipakāwi-kīsihs: October; Falling-leaves Moon

pipōn: it is winter (V-II)

pīh: (you) wait for him/her/it (V-TA)

pīhkošiton: (you) break/wreck it (V-TI)

pīhtōn: (you) wait for it (V-TI)

pīncahī: inside (PC)

pīnihš: finally (PC)

pīntik: inside/indoors (PC)

pīntikē: she/he/it is entering (V-AI)

pīš: (you) bring him/her/it (V-TA)

pītōn: (you) bring it (V-TI)

pīwāpihkōns: cents/little metal (NA)

pōni-: to stop (PV)

pōnih: (you) leave him/her/it alone (V-TA)

pōnī: she/he/it lands (V-AI)

pōsīns: cat (NA)

pwānihšimo: she/he is dancing powwow (V-AI)

s

sakahikan: nail (NI)

sawēntiwi-kīšikat: Valentine's Day; it's loving day (V-II)

sākaham: she/he/it is going outside or to the bathroom (V-AI)

sākahikan: lake (NI)

sākipakāwi-kīsihs: May; Budding Moon

sinkop: spruce tree (NA)

sīkwan: it is spring (V-II)

sīpāhahī: under (PC)

sīpi: river (NI)

sīpī: she/he/it is stretching (V-AI)

sīwihtākan: salt (NI)

skatinōwi-kīsihs: November; Freezing Moon

sōkihpon: it is snowing (V-II)

sōkihponānimat: it is blowing snow (V-II)

š

šānkahso: nine, 9

šānkahso-išihsē: it is nine o'clock (V-II)

šānkahsomitana: ninety, 90

šānkahsomitana-tahswāpik: ninety dollars, $90

šānkahso pīwāpihkōns: nine cents, 9¢

šānkahswāhk: nine hundred, 900

šānkahswāhk-tahswāpik: nine hundred dollars, $900

šānkahswāpik: nine dollars, $9

šēkisi: she/he/it is afraid/scared (V-AI)

šēmāk: right away/immediately (PC)

šikwa: and/now (PC)

šinkihšin: she/he/it is lying down (V-AI)

šīhšīp: duck (NA)

šōniyā: money (NA)

šōniyāwikamik: bank (NI)

t

tahs: but/then (PC)

tahšink: every time (PC)

taka: please (PC)

takohšin: she/he is arriving (V-AI)

takwākin: it is autumn/fall (V-II)

tānikanā: wishing (PC)

tāpiškō: just like (PC)

tēhsitiyēpiwin: chair (NI)

tēpināhk: just enough/full/any old way/carelessly (PC)

tēpwē: she/he is telling the truth (V-AI)

tēwēhikan: drum (NA)

tipahikanēns: minute; little measurement (NI)

tipahikē: she/he pays (V-AI)

tipahikēwi-kīšikat: it is pay day (V-II)

tipāhamaw: (you) pay him/her (V-TA)

tipihkahk: tonight (PC)

tipihkat: it is night (V-II)

tipihki-kīsihs: moon (NA)

tipihkonk: last night (PC)

tōtam: she/he does so (V-AI)

w

wašašk: muskrat (NA)

wāhkāhikan: house (NI)

wāhowa: geez/oh my (PC)

wāhsa: far (PC)

wāhsēnikan: window (NI)

wāhsēyā: it is sunny (V-II)

wāhtēpakāwi-kīsihs: September; Cease Blooming Moon

wāpam: (you) see him/her/it (V-TA)

wāpan: it is dawn (V-II)

wāpank: tomorrow (PC)

wāpanonk: in the east

wāpantan: (you) see it (V-TI)

wāpikanōcī: mouse (NA)

wāpikwan: flower (NI)

wāpiškā: it is white (V-II)

wāpiškisi: she/he/it is white (V-AI)

wāpōs: rabbit (NA)

wāwan: egg (NI)

wāwāhsikonēhsē: it is lightning (V-II)

wēkonēn: what (PN)

wēpahikan: broom (NI)

wēpahikē: she/he is sweeping (V-AI)

wēwēni: be careful/go slowly (PC)

wēwīp: hurry (PC)

wīcih: (you) help him/her/it (V-TA)

wīcīwākan: friend/partner (NA)

wīhahkwān: hat, cap (NI)

wīhkā: ever (PC)

wīhsini: she/he/it is eating (V-AI)

wīhsinīwikamik: restaurant (NI)

wīhtikē: she/he is marrying (V-AI)

wīn: him/her (PN)

wīnawā: them (PN)

wīnkē: really/very (PC)

wīpa: soon/early (PC)

wīyāhs: meat (NI)

Y

yoho: expression of surprise (PC)